D0611211

3/2016
STRAND PRICE
$2.00

Turn Left at the Pub

TURN LEFT AT THE PUB

by

George W. Oakes

DAVID McKAY COMPANY, INC.

New York

TURN LEFT AT THE PUB

COPYRIGHT © 1968 BY JOHN B. OAKES AS EXECUTOR
FOR THE ESTATE OF GEORGE W. OAKES

All rights reserved, including the right to reproduce
this book, or parts thereof, in any form, except for
the inclusion of brief quotations in a review.

Library of Congress Catalog Card Number: 68-19021

MANUFACTURED IN THE UNITED STATES OF AMERICA

VAN REES PRESS   •   NEW YORK

PUBLISHER'S NOTE

On January 5, 1965, the author of this book was instantly killed with his wife and son when their car plunged over an embankment on a highway near Brattleboro, Vermont. At the time of this tragic accident, Mr. Oakes had finished all the chapters contained in this book, which now stands as a fitting memorial to his love of the English countryside and as a fitting companion volume to his earlier collection of walking tours through the major cities of Europe, entitled *Turn Right at the Fountain*.

CONTENTS

Turn Left at the Pub

CANTERBURY

Canterbury has been the source and seat of Christianity in England since St. Augustine founded his mission in 597. This small Kentish city, at the end of the Pilgrim's Way, calls to mind Thomas Becket, Chaucer's *Canterbury Tales,* the medieval pilgrimages, and in a later period the Elizabethan poet, Christopher Marlowe. But Canterbury's history goes back at least a thousand years before the coming of St. Augustine.

In the Roman period a commercial community, Durovernum, grew up at this ancient ford over the River Stour. Though the name Canterbury comes from the Saxon *cant-wara-buh,* meaning "Stronghold of Men of Kent," Canterbury's appeal to today's visitor, as for the medieval pilgrim, is expressed by the city's motto with its religious connotation—"Ave Mater Angliae"—"Hail, Mother of England."

As you stroll around this once walled city, only two hours from London by road or rail, you will realize that, although the magnificent Cathedral is reason enough for your visit, Canterbury is filled with many other interesting places—the remains of St. Augustine's great abbey, one of the earliest churches in England, a remarkably well preserved tiny thirteenth-century friary, the old city wall, a Norman keep and sixteenth-century houses once occupied by Walloon and Huguenot weavers—to mention only a few.

You should start this walk through Canterbury at the massive twin-turreted **Westgate,** the historic and only remaining gateway into the city. (If you arrive by car, you'll find a car park nearby.) But before you approach the Westgate, glance at the delightful three-storied red brick Georgian building, **Westgate House,** opposite the **Falstaff Hotel.** This is the tempo-

1

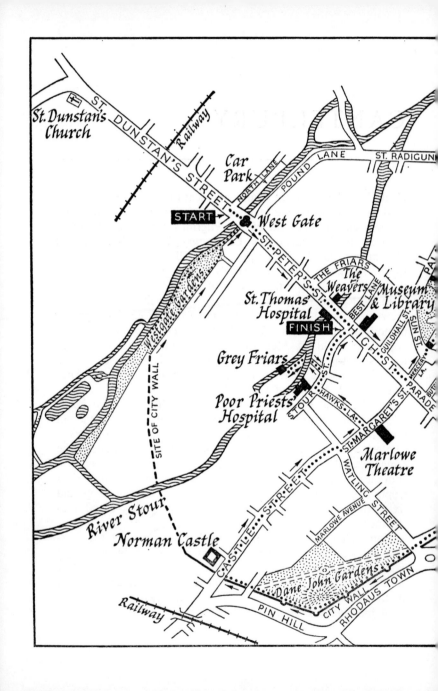

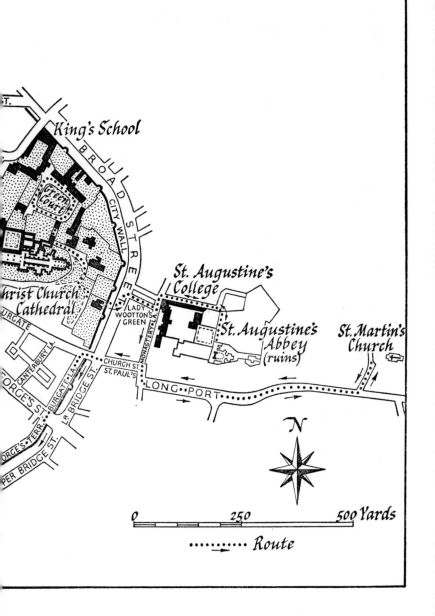

rary registry of the new **University of Kent** at Canterbury, one of Britain's newly established universities. Just as centuries ago the mingling of nearby Continental and English influences enriched the city's architecture and culture, so in future years Canterbury's intellectual life should be stimulated as its new university develops.

Rebuilt by Archbishop Sudbury about 1380 on Roman and Norman foundations, the gray stone Westgate stands at the strategic crossing of the **River Stour.** Here goods brought from the Continent and landed at Kentish ports were transported into the city. Today big double-decker buses just manage to squeeze through the narrow arch where Henry II made his way to the Cathedral "barefoot and weeping" in 1174 to do penance for the murder of Archbishop Thomas Becket. In later centuries, Chaucer and the Canterbury pilgrims probably passed through this gate.

Under the arch you will find steep stone stairs that lead to the old guard chambers, now the **Westgate Museum** (open 10:00–1:00; 2:00–6:00 except Sunday). This was the city prison from 1400–1829. You will see prisoners' cells with bits of the hangman's rope, convicts' chains and irons, an iron mantrap to catch poachers and an iron bridle to gag female scolds. The armory includes double-handed swords and shields from the time of the Crusaders, as well as a collection of constables' truncheons used by the early police forces during the Chartist riots in 1843.

From the Westgate turn right for a stroll through the **West-gate Gardens** on the banks of the Stour. At the entrance you will see on the opposite side of the river **timber and stucco houses** in characteristic Tudor style with overhanging upper stories. These were at one time inns for Pilgrims. On the corner of this row of black and white buildings is an **antiques shop,** crammed with silver, copper, brassware, and all sorts of curios. The gardens built on the foundations of the Roman walls are particularly attractive because of their fine trees (especially a huge oriental plane about two hundred years old), beautiful roses, and lawns like putting greens. Rose trellises along the river banks and the branches of the trees dipping into the stream make this one of the loveliest walks in Canterbury.

On your return to the Westgate, turn right on **St. Peter's Street** and a few minutes along this busy shopping street will bring you to **St. Thomas' Hospital.** At this point—**Kings Bridge** across another branch of the Stour—the main street is so narrow that often traffic can only move in one direction. The hospital, mainly of twelfth-century origin, was established for the benefit of pilgrims visiting the shrine of St. Thomas Becket. Go inside to see the **Norman crypt.** Look out of its windows for a delightful view of the river. Also visit the hall and the chapel.

Just across the street is one of Canterbury's most fascinating buildings—**The Weavers.** Stand on the bridge and look at these gabled half-timbered houses that rise above the river. They were built in 1500 for Walloon and Huguenot weavers who sought refuge from religious persecution in England. Go inside (open weekdays 9:00–5:00) to watch a present-day handweaver at work and then wander around the shop, which specializes in hand-woven goods and souvenirs. In the summer you can take a **boat trip** on the Stour from here.

A few yards farther along the main street (now called **High Street**) will bring you to the **Royal Museum,** popularly known as the Beaney Institute after its founder (open 9:30–12:30; 1:45–5:30). The museum's archaeological collection covers the history of Canterbury from the early stone age and contains an extensive exhibit of Roman relics, especially pottery and glass. A display upstairs of badges worn by medieval pilgrims is particularly worth seeing. In one case is a ninth-century cruciform bronze brooch, the only one of its kind in existence.

Just past the traffic signals on the right you will come to a decorative Tudor building—**Queen Elizabeth's Guest Chamber,** now a restaurant. In Tudor days, this was the state room of the Crown Inn, one of the principal inns for pilgrims. Here in 1573 Queen Elizabeth I received one of her suitors, the French Duke of Alençon. You will admire the fine sixteenth-century plaster ceiling with the initials E. R.

At the next intersection, turn left down narrow **Mercery Lane** and in a few yards you will be in a small square called the **Butter Market.** A few steps along **Burgate** to the right will bring you to **Butchery Lane.** If you'd like to see **Roman excavations,** walk along the lane to a stairway that descends below the modern building at the street level to the remains of a Roman town house with its colorful mosaic pavement and central heating chamber or hypocaust (open daily, 10:00–1:00; 2:00–6:00; Sundays, 2:00–6:00).

On returning to the Butter Market you will find several antiques and other interesting shops in the **timbered buildings** that face the majestic **Christchurch Gate,** the main entrance to the cathedral. Stand here for a few moments to study the impressive Tudor gateway, dating from 1517 and ornamented with brilliantly colored and gilded crests.

Canterbury Cathedral, spiritual home of the Anglican Church, stands near the site of St. Augustine's Cathedral which was dedicated in 602, five years after the baptism of the Saxon King Ethelbert of Kent. During the next four hundred years, a second cathedral was erected after the destruction of St. Augustine's Church only to be consumed by fire in 1067. The third and present cathedral was begun by the Norman Archbishop Lanfranc in 1070. Though much of the cathedral as it remains today was constructed during the eleventh and twelfth centuries, continued alterations and additions have taken place throughout the centuries up to the present.

Before entering the cathedral, stroll about **the precincts** a few minutes so you can appreciate the glory of its exterior, the **twin towers** at the west entrance and the magnificent 250-foot **Bell Harry Tower,** one of the finest Gothic towers ever built.

To see the cathedral properly, you should try to get a verger to take you around at least to point out the most interesting parts of the cathedral. In any case, buy a plan of the cathedral.

Starting at the **southwest entrance,** you will be impressed by the majestic sweep of the nave. Its lofty piers rising to the graceful vaulting in the roof, which is decorated by superbly carved stone bosses, one of the cathedral's great art treasures. As you walk toward the steps leading to the choir, turn back to view the **west window.** The glass in its lower tiers dates back from the late twelfth and early thirteenth century. After you pass the choir, continue along the south aisle to the **Trinity Chapel** at the eastern end of the cathedral. On the way you will pass a case with the original armor, including helmet, that belonged to the Black Prince. Up the steps in the center behind the High Altar is the Trinity Chapel. Here once stood the shrine of St. Thomas, the focus of the Canterbury pilgrimages for over three hundred years. You can see the grooves in the pavement made by the thousands of pilgrims who knelt there.

A few yards away, on the south side of the chapel, is the **brass effigy and tomb** of the Black Prince and in the circular apse, beneath the thirteenth-century glass windows portraying St. Thomas' miracles, stands **St. Augustine's marble chair.** It is used by every Archbishop of Canterbury when he is enthroned.

After you have passed along the north aisle of the choir you will come to the **northwest transept.** Here is the **Martyrdom,** the spot where Becket was murdered, commemorated by a tablet in the wall and a small slab of stone in the floor where he is supposed to have died. Take a moment to stand just a few feet away beneath the Bell Harry Tower and look up at its roof magnificently decorated in gold, red, and blue.

Before leaving the cathedral, go down to the **Norman crypt,** the largest of its kind, and the **Chapel of Our Lady of the Undercroft.** Don't miss the extraordinary figures of beasts and ape-men carved on the capitals of the pillars.

Stroll around the fifteenth-century **cloister** with its extraordinary collection of coats of arms in the vaulting, and stop in at the **Chapter House** to see its fine roof. You will see the **Archbishop's palace** just above the cloisters. His flag flies when he is in residence.

From the cloisters, turn right to the ruins of the **Monastery,** then go to the end of the sheltered walk and left to reach **Green Court,** the grounds of **The King's School.** Walk over to the entrance to the school library across the court to see the twelfth-century **Norman staircase.**

On returning from the school, you have a fine view of the

cathedral's tower. Turn left just before you reach the wall map of the cathedral, and go through an archway. After passing beside the ruins of the abbey's tall arches, you will find yourself behind the cathedral. In a moment you will be in the garden of the **Kent War Memorial,** where you get a more distant view of the cathedral.

From here go down the steps and through the **Queen's Gate** in the old city wall (note the curved battlemented stone towers nearby), then cross **Broad Street** into **Lady Wooton's Green.** In front of you is the **Missionary College of St. Augustine.** Walk straight ahead by the side of the college and in a couple of minutes you will come to the entrance to the remains of **St. Augustine's Abbey** (open 9:30–7:00 daily and Sunday in summer; until 5:30 March, April, October; closed Sunday morning rest of year). The abbey was once one of the greatest in Europe but today you can see only the ruins which, with few exceptions such as the two gates, are slightly above the ground level. However, excavations reveal the ground plan of the church and the foundations of the cloister, chapter house, dormitory, and other buildings.

Retracing your steps around St. Augustine's College, walk along **Monastery Street,** then turn left at **Longport** and after a few minutes just beyond the prison, take the first street to the left where you'll see a sign pointing to **St. Martin's Church.**

This ancient parish church at the top of a gentle slope is considered the cradle of English Christianity. St. Augustine preached here and religious services have been conducted within these walls for at least 1350 years. Most of the building is Saxon and the font predates the Norman conquest. Many of the roof beams date from the fourteenth century. After visiting this gem of a parish church with its square Saxon stone tower, wander beneath the tall yews in the quiet **churchyard.** Tall grass has overgrown many of the old tombstones. St. Martin's and its churchyard is one of the most contemplative spots in Canterbury.

On the way back from St. Martin's to Longport you pass a row of mid-sixteenth-century **almshouses.** At the end of Longport go left on **Church Street St. Paul's** by the **Eleventh Century**

Tearooms. Cross **Lower Bridge Street** and in a few yards turn left on **Burgate Lane,** past an old Tudor house with an overhanging bay window. Now cross **St. George's Street** and walk along the old **city wall. Dane John Gardens,** a pleasant park with wonderful trees, is straight ahead. Continue walking along the wall (the old **moat** is below on your left) and climb the mound for a fine view of the cathedral and the city.

At the far side of the gardens, cross **Porthgate Place** and go down a short alley to **Castle Street.** The remains of the keep of the **Norman castle,** one of the oldest in Britain, faces you. From here turn right on Castle Street for a few blocks until you reach the **Marlowe Theatre** with Tudor-style beams and brick exterior. Opposite the theatre follow **Hawks Lane** to **Stour Street,** then go right for fifty yards. You will see a sign on your left—**Grey Friars Entrance** (open 1:30–5:30 daily except Sunday).

A few minutes over a little bridge and to the left through a garden will bring you to a most picturesque spot, the little thirteenth-century Grey Friars. All that remains of this friary, the first mission of nine monks sent by St. Francis to England in 1224, is the tiny stone two-story structure built on arches spanning a branch of the Stour. Although much of the building has been restored, the original thirteenth-century roof beams and half-timber work have survived the ages. As you poke around this ancient friary and look out of its lancet window over the river gardens and the distant cathedral you may get a sense of Canterbury as it was in the days when the monastic life played such a vital role in the community.

To return to the High Street and the center of the city, just turn left a couple of hundred yards on Stour Street.

GOUDHURST

This country walk takes you into the **Weald of Kent** through scenic, rolling countryside. Orchards and hop farms fill the valley of the Teise; round, conelike oast houses with their white cowls dot the hillsides; dark green woodlands spread over much of the landscape.

You will wander through the charming village of Goudhurst perched on a hilltop with exceptional views over the surrounding country. Then you will visit ancient, moated Scotney Castle, nestling in one of the most beautifully landscaped settings imaginable, and finally go on over hill and dale to the nearby village of Lamberhurst on the River Teise. This is the soft English downland at its best.

You should do this walk on a Wednesday or Saturday afternoon between Easter and the end of October when Scotney Castle is open from 2:00–6:00. It's an "off the beaten track" tour through some of the most unspoiled country in southern England. It's not a long walk—about an hour and a quarter from Goudhurst to Scotney and another forty minutes on to Lamberhurst And you are going downhill most of the way. From Lamberhurst you can easily get a taxi for a dollar or so back to Goudhurst if you have left your car there.

The drive from London to Goudhurst probably will take about an hour and a half. If you come by train from London, it's an hour to Tunbridge Wells and then another forty minutes by bus which runs every hour except on Sunday when the bus service is every two hours. There is also an express motor coach service from Victoria Coach Station (London) which runs through the village, and also through Lamberhurst.

Goudhurst, four hundred feet above sea level, commands a fine panorama over the Weald. Its name comes from old English words and means a "good wood," so-called because the great forests that were here centuries ago produced large crops of acorns for hogs.

If you are doing the walk in the afternoon, you may want to lunch first. The **Star and Eagle,** at the top of the hill near the church, is a pleasant, timbered inn where you can get a snack in the bar or a hot lunch. The building itself dates back to the fourteenth century.

Around the corner from the Star and Eagle and opposite the church are some of the old **weavers' cottages.** Flemish weavers settled in Goudhurst during the fourteenth century and established here a prosperous cloth-making center.

Before starting down the hill, cross over to the **parish church** with its unusually short, parapeted tower. The largely fifteenth-century building has Early English perpendicular arches above which rise a fine oak-timbered roof. If you wander about the church, you will discover several rewarding fifteenth-century brasses.

On either side of the main street below the Star and Eagle are **half-timbered brick houses** with gables and tiled roofs. It's worthwhile spending a bit of time looking at the different houses and shops, for this is one of the more attractive Kentish villages. A few hundred yards will bring you to the village pond, behind which stands a **sixteenth-century house.** Note the village sign depicting hops, fruit, and oast houses, so characteristic of the surrounding farmland.

As you leave the village and make your way downhill along a path beside the road, a fine panorama unfolds before you. In about twenty minutes you will come to a road sign pointing left to Kilndown (YHA). Directly ahead is a driveway marked private drive to **Scotney Castle.** By courtesy of its owner, Christopher Hussey, noted author and authority on English country houses, you are permitted to walk on this private road, the pleasantest approach to Scotney Castle.

Soon you will cross the bridge of an old **railway line,** now out of use. Hops are growing in the fields to left and right and

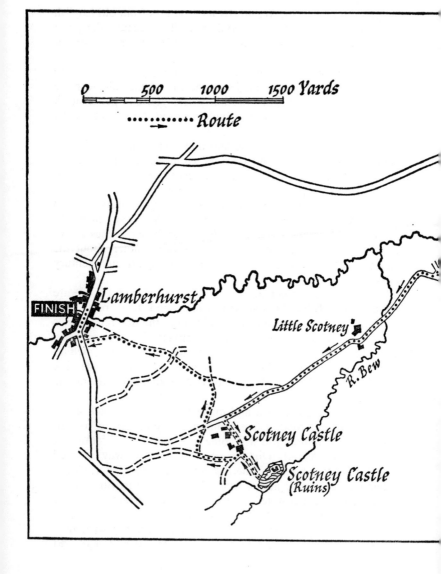

0   500   1000   1500 *Yards*

············▸ *Route*

Lamberhurst

FINISH

Little Scotney

R. Bew

Scotney Castle

Scotney Castle
(Ruins)

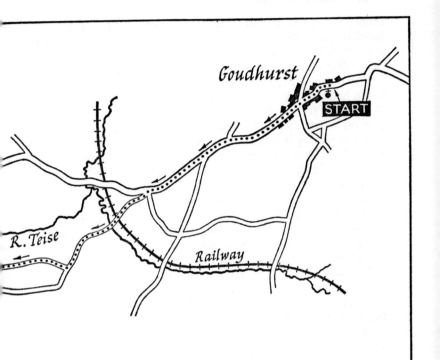

Goudhurst

START

R. Teise

Railway

N

farther along you are likely to pass sheep grazing—a typical Kentish scene. At the end of a long field go right along a dirt road, then through a gate. Farm buildings are on your right. Bear left on the farm road that runs beside a **hop field.**

You might like to have a close look at a hop vine while you're in the hop country. The hop growing season runs from the end of February to September when the vines have climbed the rigging on which they are trained to a height of about fourteen feet. The picking is usually done over a three-week period during September. Then the hops are taken to the **oast houses,** put in trays over the charcoal fire and dried. The heat of the fire passes out through the cowl or chimney at the top of the oast house, which turns with the wind. After nine or ten hours of heat, they are cooled and packed in large sacks, called pockets, for shipping to the brewery. As a consequence of drying hops by such modern methods as oil-fired burners, the old-fashioned oast houses are being replaced and often are converted into dwellings.

In a few minutes you keep left past some oast houses and about fifty yards farther go right along a road marked "No Thoroughfare—Private Road to Scotney Castle and Little Scotney Farm Only." Go round a curve on the gravel road with the farm buildings on your left. There's a church steeple coming into view on the horizon above the trees. A fine avenue of majestic, tall elms lines the road before you reach **Little Scotney Farm.** As you follow the road to the crest of the hill, you will see the new farmhouse on your right and thick woodland above the stream on your left.

Continue along the gravel road. Ignore the signs pointing to Kilndown and Lamberhurst but farther ahead go left at the sign marked "To Scotney—Private Road." This will bring you to the rear entrance of the new house with the kitchen garden on the right.

Go around to the front of the new house. Stroll over to the terrace on your right. From here you get a superb and enchanting view of the tower of the old **moated castle** and lake down below through a clearing in the thick shrubs and trees that cover the hillside. Follow the path down the hillside. As you walk along you will admire the huge rhododendron, azaleas, lime, cypress, spruce, and redwood trees. During the early summer the superb landscaping creates a brilliant and colorful palette. Few country houses can boast more tastefully planted grounds than Scotney— the result of thoughtful planning for the past hundred years.

Scotney Castle was built in 1378–1380 as a fortified house for protection against the invading French. It was later acquired by Archbishop Chichele, the founder of All Souls College, Oxford, during the fifteenth century as an endowment for his niece in whose family the castle remained until the present owner's ancestors took possession in the middle of the eighteenth century.

You pass over **stone causeways** which probably replaced timber drawbridges to enter the castle grounds. The moat or lake, filled with water lilies, surrounds two islands on one of which stands the Castle. Originally the castle had four round towers but today only one survives with traces of another. The part of the building with the high roof adjoining the round tower to the right of the entrance gates dates from the Tudor period. Note the charming balconies with leaded windows—so characteristic of Tudor days. The main portion of the house on the left was rebuilt as a three-story house before the Civil War about 1640. When the Husseys erected the new house on top of the hill, this part was taken down to form the ruin as you see it today. Great care was taken to emphasize the medieval and Tudor portions of the remaining structure. As Christopher Hussey describes it, "This is an example of the romantic interest in ruins and an interesting illustration of preserving an unwanted house by making it a ruin instead of pulling it down."

Although you cannot go inside those portions of the castle that are intact, you will enjoy sitting here by the **tall cedars** that tower over it. It's a most romantic spot with its beautifully planted grounds. Wander through the shrubs and trees along the little path that skirts the moat. There are several openings in the bushes from which you get a wonderful view of the castle above the dark waters of the moat.

Walk back up the hill through the magnificently landscaped

garden to the **new house,** which was completed in 1843. Turn again to look down on the old castle and the hillside opposite. The **cedar of Lebanon** and other trees were planted on the far slope a hundred years or so ago to create a romantic landscape picture in relation to the old tower. Christopher Hussey describes the conception of garden design at Scotney Castle as "treating the old castle and adjoining hillsides in the way that an artist composes a painting—but with vegetation, water, and masonry instead of pigments."

As you leave the new house, follow the **main drive** through the park. After passing tremendous beech trees you will shortly see a sign on a footpath to your right marked Lamberhurst. After about a hundred yards, you come to a fork in the path. Keep straight ahead and go through a gate following another sign pointing to Lamberhurst. Here you have to climb over a wooden gate into a field. Go straight up the hill to the top and toward an opening in the hedgerow. After passing through a gate you will see the village of **Lamberhurst** in the valley on the left.

Now continue ahead to the left of a hedgerow, then farther along go left again through a gate on a farm road. Soon you pass through another gate and walk along beside a field of hops. After swinging to the left around a wood, you reach the main road on which you turn right and in less than ten minutes you will cross the **River Eden** past the **George and Dragon Inn** in Lamberhurst. Just a bit farther you will see Avard Taxi Service (open daily and Sunday). From here it's only a short and inexpensive drive back to Goudhurst.

KNOLE

Knole is one of the most famous, historic, and largest baronial mansions in England. It is also among the most popular, for 30,000 visitors a year visit this accessible country house within easy reach of London. It is only about half an hour by fast train to Sevenoaks, Kent. Knole is located on the outskirts of the town and only a few minutes walk from the main street.

From Knole a pleasant walk leads through the great deer park over footpaths and country roads to Ightham Mote, a gem of a moated manor house and one seldom visited by tourists. This walk should take you about an hour and a half. From Ightham Mote it is only about half an hour or so to catch a bus to return to Sevenoaks. Or you could phone for a taxi from Sevenoaks.

Although Knole is open Wednesdays, Thursdays, Fridays, Saturdays, and Bank Holidays, 10:00–12:00; 2:00–5:00 from April–October and 10:00–12:00; 2:00–3:30 in November, December, and March (closed in January and February), if possible you should try to take this walk on a Friday when Ightham Mote is also open 2:00–5:00 in summer and 2:00–dusk the rest of the year. However, if you find you will be at Ightham Mote on another day, it is possible that a telephone call to the curator, Miss Frances Atkins (Plaxtol 380, Kent) might enable you to visit the manor house if the owner, C. H. Robinson, an American, is not in residence. In any event, it is preferable not to visit Knole on a weekend when it is likely to be quite crowded with tourists. If you happen to go on the first Wednesday in the month from April to and including September, you can also see the Knole gardens.

An excursion to Knole and Ightham Mote from London makes a delightful one-day trip. You combine interesting sight-

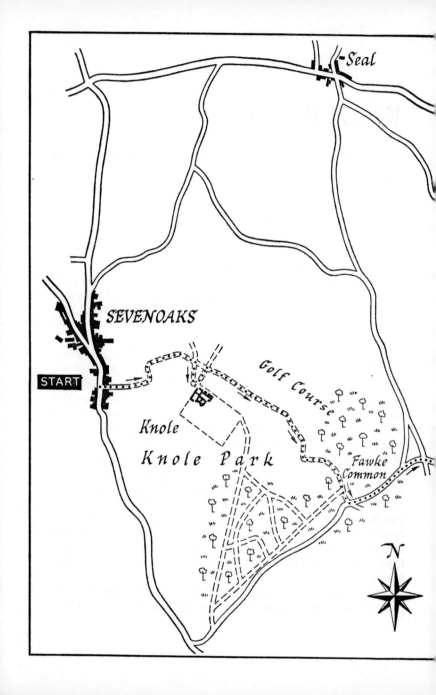

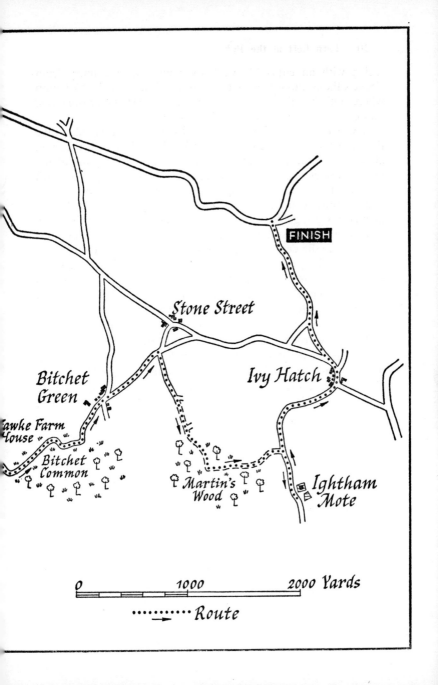

FINISH

Stone Street

Bitchet
Green

Ivy Hatch

awke Farm
Iouse

Bitchet
Common

Martin's
Wood

Ightham
Mote

0   1000   2000 Yards

••••••••→ Route

seeing with an enjoyable walk over undulating country from Knole's thousand-acre park through woods like Fawke Common where sunlight shimmers through the trees, past cherry orchards, into dark glades and on to Ightham Mote.

If you have come by train from London to **Sevenoaks,** take the bus or a taxi to the entrance to **Knole park.** It will take you about ten minutes to walk from the white wooden posts at the park gates down the hill and up the opposite slope, beneath towering trees and across the grounds to the great house. When you get close, you realize what an immense place it is. Its battlemented towers, gabled roofs with brick chimneys, and wide gray stone front are most impressive. From one of the nearby mounds you can see the depth of the building with its several courts.

In fact, Knole takes its name from the knoll on which it stands. There is a legend, mentioned by Victoria Sackville-West in her guide to Knole, that indicates its size—the house's "seven courtyards correspond to the seven days of the week, its fifty-two staircases to the weeks of the year and its three hundred and sixty-five rooms to the days of the year."

Though the earliest reference to Knole dates from 1281, much of the house was built by Thomas Bourchier, Archbishop of Canterbury, during the middle of the fifteenth century. He started the tradition of Knole's association with literary figures. During its history Knole was for a time a royal palace and has had a long connection with leading statesmen, as well as royalty, throughout the centuries.

In 1603 Knole came into the hands of Thomas Sackville as a gift of his cousin Queen Elizabeth. One of the leading statesmen of the Elizabethan reign, Sackville was the first of generations of his family who have made it the magnificent house it is today. Although a Sackville still resides at Knole, the property is now in possession of the National Trust.

You enter the house through the outer gateway, which leads into the **Green Court.** The massive, battlemented tower directly ahead, surmounted by a three-hundred year old **clock** beneath a cupola, is **Bourchier's gatehouse.** Stroll through the archway into **Stone Court.** One of the oddities in these courts are the lead **water pipes** of thirty-four different designs dating from 1605.

From Stone Court you enter the **Great Hall** where you will see a **musicians' gallery** above an elaborately carved oak **screen.** Note the great **fire-dogs** (1538) made to commemorate the marriage of Henry VIII and Anne Boleyn.

One of the most interesting rooms is the paneled **Brown Gallery** in which, besides many portraits of prominent individuals connected with Knole, you will see an outstanding and unique collection of early English furniture for which Knole is famous. From the bay window there is a good view of the grounds with its sweeping lawn and intimate rose garden.

After looking through **Lady Germain's room** and the **Spangle bedroom,** go into the old **billiard room.** Here are original billiard cues from the days of Charles I.

The **Leicester Gallery**—its floors are original—is filled with a fine collection of **Jacobean furniture.** One piece, "the Knole sofa," with adjustable drop-ends, has often been copied.

Another lavishly decorated room is the **Cartoon Gallery** named for the set of six copies of Raphael's cartoons. In the **King's Bedroom** there is an extraordinary collection of seventeenth-century silver furniture including magnificent wall sconces and a table made of wood and overlaid in silver. Look out the window for a close view of the charming garden.

On leaving the main entrance gate past two large Canadian sycamores, turn right. Beyond the car park go up the hill towards the cricket pitch. To your right are the many outbuildings —stables, brew-houses, slaughterhouses, shops for carpenters and painters—which at one time made the estate a self-contained unit.

Bear right on a narrow paved road. A bit higher up, turn around and look back at Knole. You will have a fine view of its many towers, turrets, and tall brick chimneys. The road leads across the **golf course,** which occupies much of the open space between the woods with their huge dark green trees. It is a private 18-hole course but visitors are allowed to use it. You will see herds of **Japanese deer** grazing both on the course and in the fields. Shortly the road follows a line of tall elm and oak trees. There's a small pond on the right before you come to a farmhouse. Just a bit farther on your right, there is a road lined with trees as far as you can see. This is **the chestnut walk.**

In a few yards you go out of the park through a gate. Keep left on a wide paved road that runs through a grove of trees. This delightful wood, so open and free from undergrowth, is **Fawke Common.** At the road fork ahead you bear right and follow the sign marked Stone Street. You will pass an attractive house—**Fawke Farm**—with a small rose garden. Shortly the little-traveled road runs beneath soft green mossy banks as you walk up a gradual slope.

When you get to the crossroad at **Bitchet Green,** keep straight ahead and follow the sign marked Stone Street. There's a high hedgerow on the left and an inviting cricket pitch on the right. Presently you will pass on your right a group of modern suburban houses, Broadhoath, and soon on your left a cherry orchard.

Turn right (near the road fork) on a dirt road—the public footpath to **Ightham Mote.** Continue straight ahead through an orchard and along the side of a wood. At the far side of the orchard follow the footpath sign through the trees to your right. (The farm road goes off to the left but you do not take it.) Now you go down a slope on the path through a wood and on emerging, you will be in an open draw. Follow the brook on your right. In a few minutes you will pass some old farm sheds and then you will come out on a paved road. Turn right and in a few hundred yards you will reach farm buildings with oast houses behind. Just opposite is the entrance to Ightham Mote.

Ightham Mote, set in a secluded spot at the foot of a steep hill, has all the charm and fascination you could expect of a moated fourteenth-century fortified **manor house.** It has been so carefully restored and is so well maintained that it seems almost unreal. When you first see it, you feel you have suddenly been removed from the modern world and are back in the Middle Ages.

The stone tower, sloping roofs, and brick chimneys of this rather small manor house seem to settle behind the moat into the beautifully landscaped grounds. Pause for a bit just inside the **iron gates** and study this bit of medievalism a few moments before you cross the bridge to enter the manor house through its massive oak doors. On your left as you approach the house you will notice half-timbered Tudor farm buildings and cottages.

The word *Mote* does not refer to the moat but is Saxon and indicates that the moot or council met here. The house itself dates from 1340 and was built to protect the residents from wandering robbers.

After passing under the entrance tower, you will be in the **inner courtyard.** The utter quiet of this cobblestoned court, enclosed partly by stone buildings and partly by half-timbered and stucco Tudor work, creates a romantic effect made more dramatic by the fluttering of doves above the tiled roof. The seventeenth-century **clock** with the belfry above adds a delightful touch.

The oldest part of the house just across the court is the **great hall, crypt, early chapel, and solar.** Before you enter the hall note on the outside its fine fifteenth-century window and the oriel window of the solar.

The banqueting hall itself is most impressive and has a high roof with some original oak **roof beams,** six hundred years old, and a huge seven-foot wide **fireplace.** When the hall was paneled almost a hundred years ago, and the smaller doorway was unblocked, a woman's skeleton was discovered. The story is that she had been connected with the Gunpowder plot to blow up the House of Parliament.

Above the crypt is the fourteenth-century private chapel. During the Civil War priests hid in the holes on the side of the chimney. They would climb up from the crypt through the wall and escape through the top of the chimney.

The solar or fourteenth-century ladies retiring room was so named because it was a private room where one could be quiet or solitary.

Beyond the solar you come to the Tudor chapel, built in 1520. Its **linen roll oak paneling** is a great treasure and its **barrel roof** with Tudor roses is exceptional. The panel to the left of the altar used to swing open so that priests could escape by dropping into the moat. Note the five keyholes in the heavy oak door— a means of delaying entrance into the chapel in order to allow time for priests to make their getaway.

The **drawing room** has a very fine seventeenth-century hand-painted wallpaper.

After you have toured the house, spend some time wandering about the beautifully kept lawns. At the far end, there are two huge **cedars of Lebanon.** Up the bank you will find a **waterfall** on the edge of the wood that drops down into two small oblong **ponds** on which swans, presented to the owner by the Queen's swanmaster, often are riding majestically.

After you leave Ightham Mote, turn right on the paved road. In about ten minutes you will be walking up a hill with high banks and branches of the trees making an archway overhead. Keep left at the main road and about twenty minutes after leaving the manor house you should reach the **Plough in Ivy Hatch,** an attractive pub where you can have a snack and a drink.

To catch the bus for Sevenoaks on the main road (which runs every half hour), walk past the Plough, take the right fork, and follow the sign marked Ightham Common. In about five minutes follow the sign marked Sevenoaks and Seal to the main road where you will find the bus stop.

CHIDDINGSTONE—PENSHURST

This walk in the rolling countryside of Kent will take you to the tiny renowned village, Chiddingstone, and then to an historic and intensely interesting country house, Penshurst Place. You will go through some of the loveliest, most unspoiled country in southern England. It's a walk to do on a Wednesday, Thursday, Saturday, or Sunday when Penshurst Place is open in the afternoons from 2:00–5:30 from April to the end of September.

The route is planned so that you can easily make the trip in a single day from London. If you are touring southern England, and staying in or near Penshurst, you can do the walk in the morning and visit Penshurst in the afternoon. Penshurst is quite a good center for this part of Kent—especially if you intend to visit Hever Castle or Knole. The local inn, the **Leicester Arms,** is small, comfortable, and serves good English food. Its dining room overlooks a lovely garden with a pleasant view over the nearby valley of the **River Medway** and the hills on the far side. There are only a few bedrooms, so it's wise to make a reservation. You can drive from London to Penshurst in less than an hour and a half. If you are coming by train, go to Tunbridge Wells (one hour) and take the 93 or 150 bus from the station. It runs every hour (on Sundays every two hours) and is about a twenty-five minute trip.

You should plan to begin your walk to Chiddingstone in the morning. It's not far and only will take you about an hour and a half. The footpaths are clearly marked, so you should have no trouble finding the way. If you make a late start, you can lunch in Chiddingstone, catch the frequent bus back to Penshurst from

25

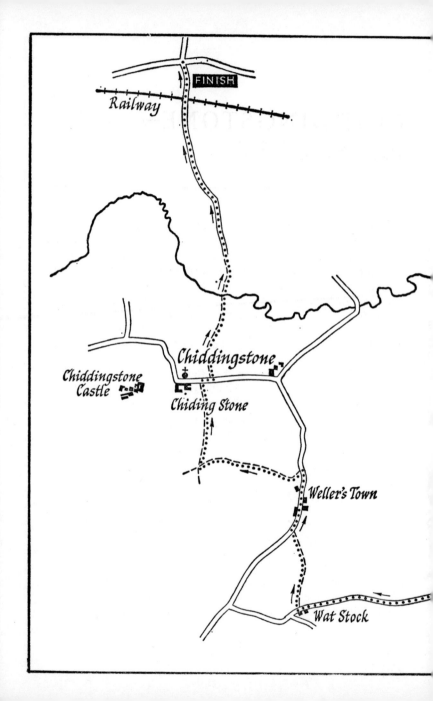

FINISH

Railway

Chiddingstone

Chiddingstone
Castle

Chiding Stone

Weller's Town

Wat Stock

0   500   1000   1500 Yards

············ Route

N

Penshurst Park

River Eden

Penshurst Place

Penshurst

START

the main road about half an hour away and visit Penshurst Place in the afternoon.

Turn left from the Leicester and take the righthand fork of the main road past the **Fir Tree House,** where you may drop in for tea later in the afternoon. You follow the road for about a hundred yards, keeping the grounds of Penshurst Place and its great park on your right.

At the sign "Public Footpath to Chiddingstone" turn left down a typically narrow, paved country lane wide enough for only one car. You are in the valley of the **River Eden.** To your right beyond the meadows and hop fields through which the river slowly winds its course you'll see shortly a long ridge of hills in the distance. Round red brick **oast houses** and the white cowls of their tapering chimneys, so characteristic of Kent, soon come into view on the crest of a hill to your right. You're not likely to meet many cars along this tree-lined tranquil lane. In a few minutes you will be reminded of the last war when you discern hidden in the brush to the right of the lane a World War II **pillbox.** You'll see many such machine gun emplacements along river valleys in southern England. They were part of the anti-invasion preparations a quarter century ago.

Near the bridge over the little river there's a sign put up by the Penshurst Angling Society to discourage poachers and off to the left you'll see a weir or dam.

Now take the right fork up a gradual hill (there's a sign to Chiddingstone on the big tree at the road junction). On your right you will pass one of those great, gnarled English oaks— its huge branches as twisted as a Van Gogh painting. Tractors in a nearby field are cutting the early summer hay beneath twin oaks that stand like sentinels. Across the fence a herd of brown Sussex cattle graze in the warm sunlight as a slight haze settles over the valley and the hills on the horizon. All of a sudden there's a sudden swoosh just ahead—a brace of partridge have taken flight. When you reach the crest of the hill, more oast houses and a church spire can be seen in the distance.

Turn left down a farm road a few yards for a view of the towers of Penshurst Place and the village church in the valley below. Return to the path and continue along the top of the hill. On your left the hedgerows are almost three feet thick and down in the flatland to your right you will see hop vines climbing up the long poles on which they ripen.

Make your way through the farmyard just ahead. You may meet one of the four workers on this 275-acre farm largely given over to the raising of beef cattle and growing of hops.

Not far ahead just beyond the curve in the road and past a small pond you go through a wooden farm gate on the right. Cross the field to the far corner and go through another gate. You'll find a signpost for the footpath back to Penshurst. Cross the road and go through the gate by the signpost marked "Public Footpath to Chiddingstone." On your right beyond a row of trees you'll see a field of hops. The path you are following runs into a dirt road. Now go through an iron gate by the signpost "Public Footpath to Chiddingstone Village" and at the end of the path along the side of a field you cross a small wooden stile. Go up the slope through the field and walk between two large oak trees, then cross another stile at the far side. On your left you will notice one of those magnificent English oaks with tremendous branches and thick foliage—the kind of oak that stage designers have in mind when creating the Windsor Forest set for the opera *Falstaff*. As you go out through the gate from the footpath on to the road, the bells of Chiddingstone Church may be striking the hour. The village of Chiddingstone is only a couple of hundred yards down the road to your left.

An interesting and unusual sign behind a bench on the left of the road reads as follows:

"A Request from The Holiday Fellowship"

"Friend when you stray or sit and take your ease,
On Moor, or Fell, or under spreading trees,
Pray leave no traces of your wayside meal
No paper bag, no scattered orange peel,
Nor daily journal littered on the grass;
Others may view these with distaste and pass,

Let no one say and say it to your shame
That all was beauty here until you came."

These words printed on a card can be obtained from the Holiday Fellowship, Fellowship House, Great North Way, Hendon, London N.W. 4.

On your left you will notice a sign "To the Chiding Stone" so take the footpath for about a hundred yards, go over a stile and shortly you will come to a large outcrop of sandstone. The lower part is in the shape of a seat. There is a story that the Druid priests in ancient times used to chide the people from this stone, which also resembles a pulpit.

A few moments down the road will bring you to the little village of **Chiddingstone**—a remarkably preserved row of Tudor half-timbered houses on the left and the parish church on the right. This group of gabled stucco houses with overhanging second stories (many date from the middle of the fifteenth century) isn't marred by other buildings of a later period. The whole effect of this unique village is much as it was during the days of Elizabeth I. At the far end of the village (only a couple of hundred yards long) is the **Castle Inn** where you can get a snack or a proper lunch.

Tall yews line the path to the **parish church** mostly built in the middle of the fourteenth century. Wander around the church and then stroll about the **old churchyard** shaded by a magnificent cedar. The National Trust now has presented Chiddingstone as an unspoiled and unrivaled picture of the past.

To catch the Penshurst bus, go back along the road you came for fifty yards beyond the church and turn left at a sign marked "Public Footpath." After passing through a gate, you go down the hill on a paved footpath, then through another gate and across a field. Now cross the **River Eden** (there's another pillbox on the right) and shortly you'll pass a gay garden on your right and a charming house on the left. Now you are following a dirt road and after passing through another gate you will see **Chiddingstone Castle** and **Chiddingstone Church** way off across the fields on your left. Canterbury sheep with their lambs may be grazing in the nearby field. Continue on this lane, over the railway bridge, through a farmyard and past some oast houses until you reach Route B2027. The Penshurst bus (Penshurst is to your right), which runs every hour (Sundays every two hours) will stop just across the road if you signal it.

On returning to the Leicester Arms, stroll along the village street a few yards to the right and turn left to the **post office,** a part of the village store. You will find it entertaining to have a few words with the postmistress, Mrs. Eagleton. Her husband's family have lived in Penshurst since 1820. The post office faces a courtyard of half-timbered buildings. It is called **Leicester Square** and the local residents like to claim it is the original Leicester Square because some of the cottages date from the fourteenth century before the London square existed. Nearby you will notice the office of the National Provincial Bank—it is open only 10:00–11:30 on Thursday as is customary in small villages.

Stroll under the arch and through the churchyard. Have a look through the parish church before continuing along the path to the park. Although the church is largely fifteenth century, the arches on the north side date from 1200. In addition to interesting **brasses,** there are several monuments to the Sidney family.

In a moment or two the battlemented towers and long, low gray stone buildings of Penshurst Place suddenly come into view on the right when you come out of the wood. As you walk to the entrance on the far side, glance to your left towards the sloping hills that lead to Chiddingstone. The great bushy trees, the vast expanse of fields and the grazing sheep provide a picturesque setting for this six-hundred-year-old country house, one of the most historic, interesting, and beautifully situated in all of England.

Penshurst Place is another great house rich in historic and literary associations, the chief being the fact that Sir Philip Sidney, the Elizabethan soldier and poet, was born here in 1554. Penshurst Place has been in the possession of the Sidney family ever since King Edward VI gave it to Sir William Sidney, grandfather of Sir Philip, in 1552. The present owner, Viscount De L'Isle and Dudley, is a collateral descendant of Sir Philip.

Though the main character of Penshurst Place is Elizabethan, the fine **great hall** in this stately mansion dates from 1340—which makes it older, even, than Westminster Hall in London. After crossing the large court, inside the towered gateway, you will come to this most impressive chamber. You cannot help but be struck by the great proportions of the Hall and the height of its timbered roof. Many original fourteenth-century beams have survived. The two long tables in the Hall are fifteenth century.

As you go through the house, be sure to see the crested **helmet** that was carried at the funeral of Sir Philip Sidney, the **state sword** of Queen Elizabeth I's friend Robert Dudley, Earl of Leicester, and a **bronze bushel measure** made from cannon captured from the Spanish Armada. The oak paneled **Long Gallery** with its great collection of sad-faced portraits, including those of Queen Elizabeth I and her favorite, the Earl of Leicester, is a fine example of domestic architecture in the late sixteenth and early seventeenth centuries. Glance out of the mullion windows for a lovely view of the gardens and valley of the Medway.

After touring the house, spend some time strolling about the beautifully **landscaped gardens.** The high clipped yew hedges, luxurious herbaceous borders with marvelous light and dark blue delphinium, and the exquisite roses are some of the most attractive features of the gardens. An architectural pattern of walks and flower beds around a central **lily pond** is closest to the house and conforms to its formal style.

To return to the village, go to the far corner of this formal garden and you will find a door that lets you out of the grounds. A few yards to your right will bring you back to Leicester Square.

MIDHURST

This walk is planned for the tourist who would like to spend a day walking in unspoiled, beautiful country, not far from London—without doing much sightseeing. You won't visit any country houses or cathedrals (only a few parish churches), but you will be in some of the loveliest countryside to be found in southern England.

Starting in the small town of Midhurst in West Sussex, almost at the foot of the South Downs, you will walk to five neighboring and tiny villages—Woolbeding, Stedham, Iping, Chithurst, and Trotton in the enchanting valley of the **River Rother.** This rolling landscape, partly wooded, partly divided by hedgerows into open fields, dotted here and there with farmhouses, has that soft, intimate quality only found in England.

If you want to go somewhere near London on a Sunday for a day's walk in the country, it's just an hour by train to Haslemere on the Portsmouth line. From there you can take a taxi and in about twenty minutes be in Midhurst. Or you can go by frequent bus service from Haslemere to Midhurst. By car, Midhurst is about an hour and a half from Hyde Park Corner. If you are touring southern England, Midhurst is right on the route between Tunbridge Wells and Chichester or Winchester.

Though you are quite close to London, the Rother valley is not a tourist center and so is not crowded even on weekends. Midhurst itself attracts many people because of the polo on Saturday and Sunday, but few polo enthusiasts know about the nearby villages.

This walk from Midhurst through some of the most charming villages in Sussex will probably take you three or four hours at an easy pace. It's not hard walking—most of the time you are

33

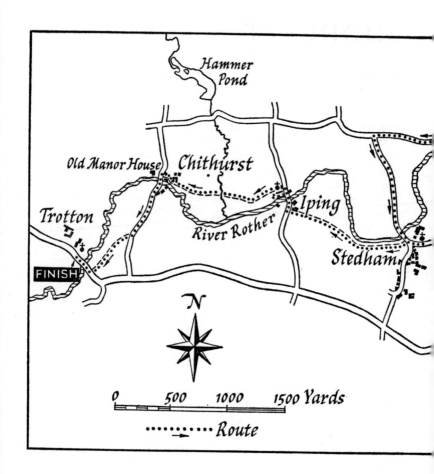

Hammer
Pond

Old Manor House   *Chithurst*

Trotton

Iping

River Rother

Stedham

FINISH

N

0   500   1000   1500 Yards

·········· → *Route*

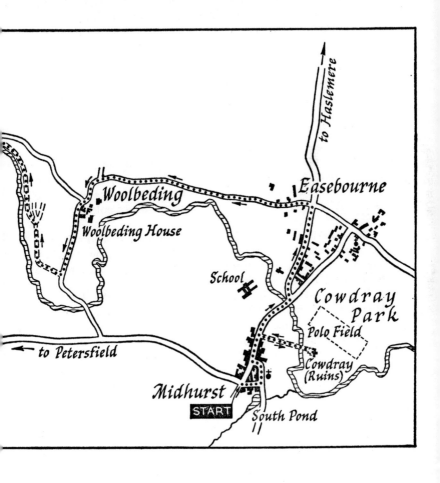

to Haslemere

Woolbeding

Woolbeding House

Easebourne

School

Cowdray
Park

Polo Field

to Petersfield

Cowdray
(Ruins)

Midhurst

START

South Pond

on footpaths in the low land of the river valley. However, ladies should wear wide skirts or slacks and low-heeled shoes. The bus service from Petersfield to Midhurst, stopping at Trotton, runs every two hours daily and Sunday, so you should not have any trouble returning. Also if you wish to cut the length of the walk, you are only a few hundred yards from the bus route in either Iping, Chithurst, or Stedham. From these bus stops on the Petersfield-Midhurst road you can pick up a bus to Midhurst every hour, including Sundays.

If you do take this walk on a weekend in the summer, you could plan to be back in Midhurst in time to watch the exciting polo matches in which the Duke of Edinburgh frequently plays. These take place at **Cowdray Park** on Saturday and Sunday at 3:15 between early May and the end of August. Often the Queen drives over with the Duke to watch the polo. The standard here is unusually high. You are not likely to see better polo anywhere in England.

Midhurst is a quaint little village. It has many Tudor houses with oak beams, stucco fronts, and overhanging upper stories. The name Midhurst is probably of Saxon origin, meaning the town in the middle woods.

You should start in the **Market Square** by the **Elizabeth House,** a half-timbered Tudor house now a tearoom. (You can leave your car in the car park in the square.) Stroll a few yards along **West Street,** then turn right into **Wool Lane** to see a row of interesting Tudor buildings overhanging the narrow street. The **Spread Eagle,** an inn dating back to 1430, at one time known for its good food, is on the corner opposite the Elizabeth House.

On returning to the square, you will find on your right of the car park an iron grill beneath the steps of the old **Town Hall.** Look carefully and you will see the town's stocks and pillory behind the grill.

Stroll up the street past the **parish church** where the curfew has been rung nightly at eight o'clock for centuries. Continue to the stucco and timber houses of **Knockhundred Row** around the corner after the main street makes a left turn. A few yards further and you will be in **North Street.** Either now or later on you may want to do some window shopping for there are many antiques shops in Midhurst.

Go right on North Street, a wide street with several interesting red brick houses on the left, including the **Georgian building** occupied by the council offices. The **Angel Hotel** on the right is one of the ancient inns where the Pilgrim Fathers rested en-route to Southampton. Stop in at the bus office a little further along to check the latest bus schedules between Trotton and Midhurst before starting off on your walk. The large gray stone building on the left is the **grammar school,** one of whose famous students was H. G. Wells.

Take the footpath to the right of North Street for a few hundred yards to the ruins of **Cowdray Castle.** Although you cannot wander about the ruins, it is worth taking a few minutes to see them. Built in 1530, Cowdray was one of the finest manor houses in the country. A fire at the end of the eighteenth century destroyed most of the building except the west front and its battlemented Tudor gatehouse. The polo field is just beyond the castle ruins, which provide a picturesque backdrop for the matches.

Returning to North Street, turn right. The secondary modern school, opened in 1951—a long low brick building with large windows—is on your left. After crossing the River Rother, turn left on the Haslemere road into the village of **Easebourne,** which once was more important than Midhurst. Take the path that runs above the road. Shortly you pass the village cricket ground on your left.

At the first crossroads, go left, following the sign to Wool-beding. High hedgerows line the narrow road and the branches of spreading trees overhang it. The gnarled trunk of a great oak stands on the right. You keep on straight ahead past an attractive farmhouse. Rambler roses cover the walk. Shortly there is an opening in the hedgerow on your left. Stop for a moment to enjoy the wonderful view—the wheat in the foreground blowing in the wind, the open fields and rows of trees in the valley, and the long ridge of the **South Downs** on the horizon. Note the huge beech tree on your right as the road goes down a slope between high banks on either side.

Just beyond the road junction you pass on your left **Wool-beding House,** a large house built about 1770 and set back from the road down a wide drive bordered with flowers. The adjoining farm buildings are quite interesting with their high stone walls and gabled roofs. Woolbeding was described in the Domesday Book as "a perfect manor containing a church, mill, meadow and wood." Only the mill has disappeared in the course of many centuries. The **parish church,** behind a high stone wall right near the house, is thought to be partially of Saxon construction. A row of huge yew trees stands in the churchyard.

Walk along the road lined with fine oak trees to the village cricket pitch on your left in a picturesque setting with the wooded hills behind. Now retrace your steps past Woolbeding House and turn left at the road junction. Continue on this narrow country lane, keeping left at the next intersection, until you come to a paved road that goes to the left. Go down here past farms until you reach **Stedham Bridge.** The diamond-shaped stone buttresses and old arches of this stone bridge are very picturesque. Cross Stedham Bridge and bear left past a timbered house that dates from medieval days. The name Stedham is Saxon and means "homestead." As you approach the **parish church,** you will see a remarkable **yew** in the churchyard with a 35-foot circumference. It may be 900 years old. All that remains of the church, built in 1040, is the lower part of the tower of Saxon construction. Inside there is a thirteenth-century oak chest and a 1660 copy of the Book of Common Prayer.

Return toward the bridge but just before you reach it, go left on a footpath. An arbor of trees covers the path until you reach an open meadow where you get a fine view of the distant hills. Go through a gate below a big chestnut tree, then walk close to a hedgerow. Shortly you will come to a narrow footpath which you follow across a field in which there are several fine trees that stand alone. A gate at the far end of the field leads into a path that in a few yards will bring you down a slope to the paved road in **Iping.**

Turn right on the road past E. and G. Eade, timber merchants, on your left and cross the seventeenth-century **stone bridge,** similar to the one at Stedham and only wide enough for one car.

Follow the public footpath behind the church and between a farm building and the new burial ground. Then climb over a wooden fence and cross the meadow to a gate on the far side. You go over a stile and at the end of the field cross a little footbridge over a brook. Keep straight ahead through the next field alongside a barbed wire fence. Farther on you cross a stile on the south side of a farm building and continue across the field to the main buildings of **Chithurst Farm.** Just through the gate you will find a paved road.

A few steps across the road to the right will bring you to **Chithurst Church.** This tiny stone church was built in the eleventh century and was mentioned in the Domesday Book. The entire building, except for the porch, is pre-Tudor. You will find this an exceptionally charming little parish church, almost a chapel. In the churchyard are some tombstones with double crosses which may date back to the twelfth century. Just behind the church the fifteenth-century **manor house,** an attractive Tudor building, stands on a mound overlooking the Rother. Nearby is an ancient **spring** that was mentioned in the Domesday Book.

Turn right from the church and cross the bridge over the Rother. At the entrance to the house on your left you will see **palm trees,** an indication of the mild climate England enjoys despite occasional bad winters.

Walk along the road and just beyond **White's Farm** on the right you will notice a low gray electric transformer behind a large tree. Take the footpath that runs alongside the field. Cross an old stile and go through a field as far as a barbed wire fence. Turn left along the fence to a large oak, then cross an old wooden bridge. This will bring you in front of a large house, **Trotton Place.** Turn right and you will be behind **Trotton Church.** Go through the gate on the right and skirt the seventeenth-century house. A gate near the house will take you to the entrance of **St. George Church.**

The **West Tower** is the oldest part of the church and dates from about 1230. The interior is remarkably spacious, particularly for a Gothic church of this size. The nave and chancel were built about 1300. The fine wooden roof, including several of the original timbers, is about a hundred years later. Be sure to see two outstanding **brasses.** The earlier one (about 1310) of Margaret de Camoys in the floor of the nave is the earliest brass of a woman anywhere. The other brass in the chancel, done a century later, is one of the finest in England. A magnificent work, it is in almost perfect condition. It depicts Lord Camoys, who commanded the left wing at the Battle of Agincourt, and his wife. On the west wall you will see fourteenth-century **wall paintings** showing the Seven Deadly Sins and the Seven Acts of Mercy.

Just outside the church is the bus stop where you can catch the Midhurst bus. If you have any time to spare, walk to the left down the road a few hundred yards, cross another ancient stone bridge and stop in at **The Keeper's Arms,** a pub on the slope to your right. Here you can have a snack, a drink, and sit in the pleasant little garden above the Rother valley until it is time to return to Midhurst.

CHICHESTER

The cathedral city of **Chichester,** one of the most interesting and attractive places in southern England, lies in the flat country between Sussex's South Downs and the sea. The tiny village of **Bosham** (pronounced Bozzam), a sailing center on one of the bays in Chichester harbor, is so much on the water's edge that the high tides lap the houses and flood some streets.

This walk combines town and country. First you tour in main streets and quiet lanes the historic and artistic corners of Chichester from its twelfth-century cathedral and other medieval buildings to its fine Georgian houses. Then, as a change from this busy market town, you walk on roads and footpaths for about an hour and a half to Bosham, one of the most charming and secluded spots you will find on the south coast. You can return quickly to Chichester by bus, leaving Bosham every hour at 34 minutes past the hour daily, and on Sunday there is service every two hours on even hours. Both these walks can be done easily in one day without hurrying—Chichester in the morning and Bosham in the afternoon.

Chichester's origins go back to the days of Roman occupation when it was called Noviomagus. But its present name comes from the Saxon period. The Roman town was conquered by the Saxon Chieftain Aella who gave it to his son Cissa and so it became Cissa's camp and thus Chichester.

The Roman influence is reflected in the plan of the city, with four main streets and city walls. **The walls,** which circle the old town for a mile and a half, are built on Roman foundations though the visible sections are largely medieval.

Begin your stroll through Chichester at the town's center, the **Market Cross,** the junction of the four streets, appropriately

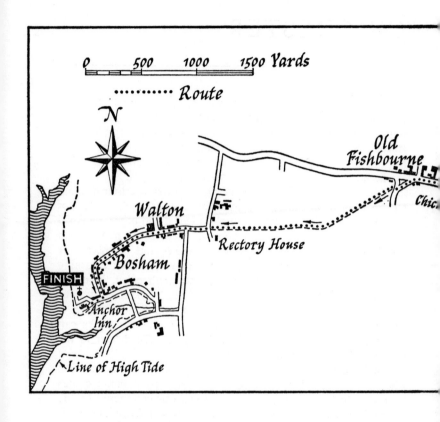

0   500   1000   1500 Yards

·········· Route

N

Old
Fishbourne

Walton

Chic.

Rectory House

Bosham

FINISH

Anchor
Inn

Line of High Tide

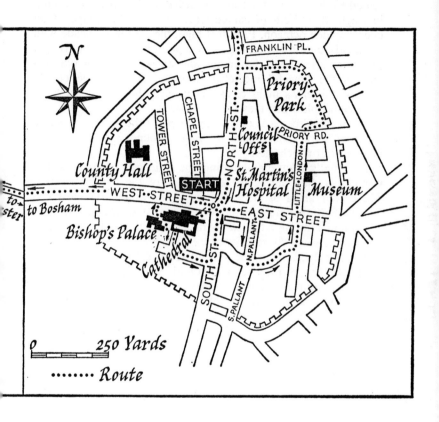

N

County Hall

to Bosham

to ...ster

TOWER STREET

CHAPEL STREET

FRANKLIN PL.

Priory Park

NORTH ST.

Council Offs

PRIORY RD.

START

St. Martin's Hospital

LITTLE LONDON

Museum

WEST STREET

EAST STREET

Bishop's Palace

Cathedral

SOUTH ST.

S. PALLANT

N. PALLANT

0 — 250 Yards

.... Route

named North, South, East, and West. The graceful cross, presented to the city in 1501 and regarded as the finest of its kind
in England, is built of carved Caen stone in the shape of an
open-arcaded octagon. Fifty feet high, the elaborate facade with
its shields and other decoration, is supported by huge buttresses.
Pinnacles rise above the arches and an octagonal cupola sur-
mounts the graceful medieval structure. Beneath the cupola
there is the city's main clock. Years ago the arcade sheltered
country people when they came to town.

From the Cross it is only a few steps to the **cathedral** whose
277-foot spire can be seen for miles around and is the chief
landmark of Chichester.

Essentially a Norman building, the main part of the cathedral
was constructed during the early years of the twelfth century.
The double aisles of the **nave,** one of the cathedral's most distinctive features, make it one of the widest in the country. As
you wander around the cathedral, you will be struck by the
contrast between the severity of the nave and the rich decoration
behind the **High Altar.** Be sure to see nearby Graham Suther-
land's **painting** of the risen Christ with St. Mary Magdalene. In
the south choir aisle are two magnificent twelfth-century **sculptures** representing the raising of Lazarus and Christ at the Gate
of Bethany. These are described as "the finest medieval carvings
to be found in the country." While you are looking about the
choir with its fine early English work and the **Bishop's Throne,**
don't miss the beautifully carved **misericord seats.** The cathedral
also possesses an unusual collection of **portraits,** many painted
on wood. Outside the **West Door** you will see the cathedral's
perpendicular **bell tower,** the only detached one in England. It
is just a step from the West Door to the cathedral's **Prebendal
School** which has a most delightful **garden.**

The fifteenth-century **cloisters** with their fine roof enclose a
burial ground known as the **Paradise.** At the end of the cloisters
turn down charming **St. Richard's Walk** to a delightful part of
the precinct. There is a quiet, other-worldly air along these
walks behind the cathedral. **Medieval and Georgian houses,**
with their flower-covered walls, big trees, and tastefully planted

gardens, make this part behind the cathedral one of the most delightful sections of Chichester. Though you are only yards from the busy main streets and shopping area, you seem to be miles away as you poke about these fascinating corners of the close.

Starting down St. Richard's Walk from the cloisters, the **flint building** on your left (No. 1) is the house of the Wiccamical Prebendaries and dates from the fourteenth century. No. 2, an eighteenth-century house, is most attractive. High stone walls line the walk to **Canon Lane.** Just across is **The Deanery,** a distinguished red brick eighteenth-century house. Turn right along Canon Lane for a few yards to the fourteenth-century gatehouse of the **Bishop's Palace.** If you step through the arch for a few moments you will see the large stone Palace, part of which was built in the thirteenth century. A tall cedar of Lebanon shades the courtyard and behind it rises the cathedral spire. A glance to your left reveals the Palace's extensive **gardens** just beyond the crenelated stone wall.

Now stroll down Canon Lane beneath high stone walls and past the Deanery. The building on your right is the **Residentiary,** mostly of the sixteenth century. Farther down on the right is the thirteenth-century **Chantry,** older than any other domestic building in Chichester. On your left before you go through the thirteenth-century Canon Gate to South Street, you will find the **Vicars' Close** with four fifteenth-century houses.

Turn left in **South Street** past some interesting shops. In a few moments you will come to the **Vicars' Hall and Undercroft.** Go down into the Undercroft, now called the Crypt Coffee Shop, for a snack or lunch. You'll find it quite amusing to eat in this vaulted twelfth-century crypt which, next to the Cathedral, is the "oldest visible remnant of medieval architecture in the city." It is believed that the crypt or undercroft was part of one of the ancient Guildhalls. Go upstairs for a look at the fourteenth-century Vicars' Hall with its **open timber roof.**

Stroll up South Street for another look at the Market Cross, then go right on **East Street** to the **supermarket** on the corner of North Pallant. If you haven't had a chance to compare an English supermarket with yours at home, now is your opportunity.

Turn right on **North Pallant. The Pallants**—North, South, East, and West—are a miniature version of Chichester's streets of the same name. The word "Pallant" comes from the Latin "palantia" meaning exclusive jurisdiction and signifies the fact that the Archbishop of Canterbury had such rights in this area until the middle of the sixteenth century. As you stroll down North Pallant you'll see that the houses on this and the other Pallants are of unusually fine proportions with most attractive doorways, windows, and window boxes filled with flowers. Few of these houses are still private residences. Most were erected during the eighteenth and early nineteenth centuries. The large brick house at the corner of North and East Pallant is **Pallant House,** built in about 1712. It is familiarly known as Dodo House, from the stone ostriches, the crest of the original owner, which stand perched on the brick gatepiers.

Go left on **East Pallant** and again left on **Baffin Lane.** Cross East Street to a narrow street called **Little London** along which are several distinctive eighteenth-century houses.

At the corner of East Row stands the relatively new **City Museum** in a white brick eighteenth-century building (open weekdays, 10:00–6:00 April–Sept.; open Tuesday–Saturday, 10:00–5:00 October–March; closed Sunday).

The museum's collection covers the history of Chichester from prehistoric times to the present. Its well displayed exhibits include an extensive collection of Roman relics—vases, coins, glass, jewelry, etc.—as well as many pieces from the Saxon and medieval periods of the city's history. You can also see the original city stocks last used in the nineteenth century, a fascinating diorama of the Battle of Quebec in which the Royal Sussex regiment fought, plus regimental uniforms, regalia, and medals. A piece of modern sculpture by John Skelton, a symbol of discovery, stands in the museum's forecourt.

From the museum continue along Little London to **Priory**

Road where you turn right past a fine mansion and cross into the park. Keep to your right along the park and go up on the walk that runs along the top of the **old city wall.** It's a delightful stroll under the trees with a park on either side. In a few minutes you will pass a high grassy mound, the remains of Chichester Castle.

After swinging around the curve of the wall, turn left past the bowling green. The stone building set back on the lawn is **Greyfriars,** the thirteenth-century chancel of the friars' church. It houses the collections of the old museum and is open to the public.

Leave the park through the gates, go down **Guildhall Street** and in fifty yards you will be at **North Street.** The fine Georgian house on your right is the **Ship Hotel.** If you were to go right on North Street for about ten minutes or so, you would come to the **Chichester Festival Theatre** where Sir Laurence Olivier directed the National Theatre in the opening productions. John Clements now directs the theatre and it has attracted international attention during the summer seasons. The theatre itself, located in **Oaklands Park,** is a hexagonal modern building of unusual design.

A few yards to the left along North Street from Guildhall Street will bring you to the **Council House** with its open arcade over the sidewalk. Before you go in, notice the famous **stone** with an inscription dedicating a temple to Neptune and Minerva, an important relic of Roman days. The facade of the eighteenth-century brick building with its white Ionic columns has a particularly graceful air. The spacious **Council Chamber** on the first floor (open 11:00–1:00; 2:00–4:30 daily in July and August) is an elegant example of eighteenth-century design. You'll be interested to see the city's silver-gilt mace, the corporation plate as well as royal charters to the city, including an ancient one granted by King Stephen in 1135.

Turn right from the entrance to the Council House and go down **Lion Street** to **St. Martin's Square.** Across the square is **St. Mary's Hospital.**

This thirteenth-century hospital, still used as a home for aged women, has preserved its medieval character—perhaps more so than any similar institution in England. (Open 11:00–12:00; 2:00–5:00, April 1–September 30; 2:00–4:00, October 1–March 31; closed Sunday.) The interior is most impressive. You will be fascinated by the high, massive roof of thirteenth-century timbers, the **great hall** where the inmates live in small cubicles and the chapel with its carved **misericord seats.** An original carved oak **screen** divides the chapel from the hall. Go into the adjacent **garden** for a good view of the great sloping roof that almost reaches to the ground, making the entire building look like a medieval barn. The buildings of the hospital resemble, on a smaller scale, those at the hospital in Baune

After you have visited the hospital and its adjacent **alms-houses,** go along St. Martin's Street to East Street and then left to return to the Cross.

Begin your walk to **Bosham** here at the Cross and head along West Street past the cathedral and County Hall. As you leave the center of town you will pass suburban-type homes with attractively planted gardens. If you happen to be here in late June, delphinium and roses should be in bloom. Cross the railway line and continue along the main road through **New Fishbourne.** Keep straight ahead at the double carriage-way and go past two pubs, the **Woolpack** and the **Bull's Head.** Just beyond the **Black Boy,** another pub, bear left on a paved lane. In about fifty yards follow a footpath to the left of a row of poplar trees. After passing a pond and leaving a farm road to your right, cross a stile and your path continues straight ahead. You should see the spire of **Bosham Church** ahead of you and a bit to the left. Approximately seven hundred yards from the pond should bring you out at a bend on a paved road. To reach **old Bosham,** walk on in the same direction until you come to the **Berkeley Arms** and then bear left past a thatched cottage. As you walk along, you'll be struck by the number of simple houses that can boast attractive gardens with fragrant roses. When you reach the little village you'll see a sign at the water's edge, "Road Flooded by Tide"—a warning that motorists should heed for there's a fourteen-foot tide here. Cars parked on or just off the road are frequently stranded in a very short time when the tide is rising.

Turn right along a narrow street lined with charming cottages, some of which are built right above the high water line. In a moment you will reach the **Anchor Bleu,** a pub that's open from 10:00–2:30 on weekdays, and 12:00–2:00 and 7:00–10:30 on Sunday, where you can get bread, cheese, sandwiches, and beer.

Looking out of the pub window just above the high water, you'll see swans swimming outside and trim sailboats riding at anchor. You're quite likely to strike up a conversation with old sailors. Some of them tell exciting tales of their wartime experiences. Also, there's an amusing weather vane, which the pub owner made, that shows by electric indicators and lights from which direction the wind is blowing.

Around the corner from the pub you will come to the **village church.** Built by the Saxons on Roman and British foundations, this church stands on "the oldest site of Christianity in Sussex" where God was worshipped 250 years before St. Augustine came to Canterbury. You'll see stones from the Roman basilica at the foot of the fine **chancel arch** which appears in the Bayeux Tapestry. Just to the right is the **tomb** of King Canute's daughter buried here in 1020. The interior is a mixture of Saxon, Norman, and early English.

Just beyond the church you will find the **quay** where yachtsmen may be readying their boats. This is a good spot to sit. Look out over the harbor and enjoy this nautical scene. There is a sign on the dock of the **Bosham Sea School** and a few yards away you will see sailboats being wheeled from the property of the **Bosham Sailing Club.**

When the tide recedes, you can walk along the gravel bottom beside the pub and adjacent cottages that look out over the harbor. At low tide the grassy reeds stand up above the little water that remains between this side of the creek and the opposite shore a quarter mile away. When you turn up from the water's edge to stroll to the bus stop in the village, you'll find cars in the road that only an hour or so earlier were completely under water. As you leave Bosham to return to Chichester, you'll agree that its old church, water-side location, and jolly pub make it one of the most picturesque and peaceful villages on the south coast.

SALISBURY

To walk from **Salisbury Cathedral** to **Wilton House** is to move
from the spiritual world of the thirteenth century to the gay,
amusing life of an English country house in the days of the
Tudors and Stuarts. When you stroll around the tranquil cathedral close, still a haven of meditation and repose as it has been
for seven hundred years, and look up at the glorious spire soaring above the magnificent mass of Gothic architecture, you sense
that the inspiration which created this superb structure lives on.
Nowhere in England has the spirit of the Middle Ages survived
more successfully the violent vicissitudes and changes of seven
centuries than here in the close of Salisbury Cathedral. Salisbury
is the only one of the great English cathedrals that is set in such
lovely and extensive grounds that you can stand from afar—
as did the artist John Constable—and appreciate its full glory.

The walk from Salisbury to Wilton is thoroughly delightful.
You stroll through the long meadows by the River Nadder and
frequently get picturesque views of the cathedral. It is a short
distance, too, and should only take you an hour and a half or
so. When you reach Wilton you will visit one of the most interesting country houses in England and one that is located in a
beautiful park. This walk combines Salisbury Cathedral, several
interesting places in Salisbury itself, an excursion into pleasant
country, and a fascinating country house.

You can easily reach Salisbury from London by road or rail.
It is quickest to take the fast train from Waterloo (most carry
restaurant cars) and you will be in Salisbury in about an hour
and three-quarters. Should you be touring southern England,
Salisbury is likely to be on your route. If you are arriving at or

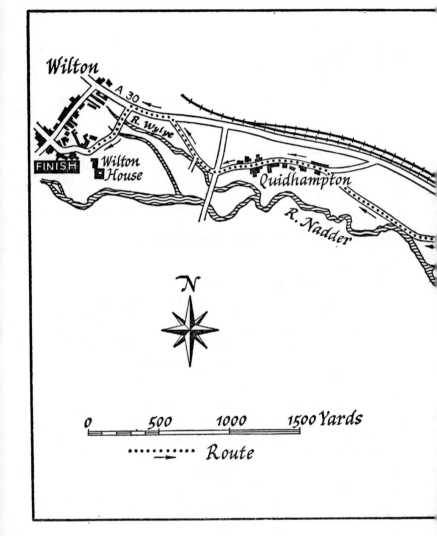

Wilton

A 30

R. Wylye

FINISH

Wilton
House

Quidhampton

R. Nadder

N

0   500   1000   1500 Yards

Route

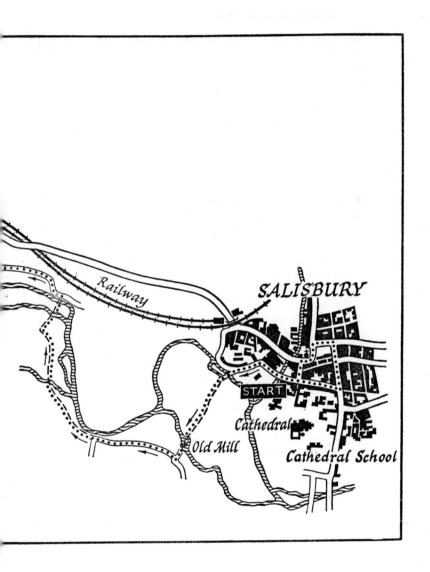

sailing from Southampton, Salisbury is only twenty-two miles away.

When you are driving to Salisbury, the Cathedral's lofty spire, a famous landmark in this part of the country, will be visible for miles around as it is the focus of the city.

On arrival in the town, go directly to the **cathedral close** where there is a parking area. Pause for a few moments by the green to absorb the mood of this lovely scene—the lines of the great gray Gothic cathedral, its lofty **spire** that rises over four hundred feet (the highest church spire in England), the broad expanse of lawn encircled by a fourteenth-century stone wall, and the charming Georgian brick houses that surround the spacious close.

The most perfectly proportioned example of early English Gothic style, Salisbury Cathedral is an architectural classic. The only English cathedral of uniform design, it was begun in 1220 and completed thirty-eight years later. The tower and spire are fourteenth century.

After strolling about the close to view the cathedral from different angles, enter through the **north door.** At once you will be struck by the somber effect of the interior—perhaps due to the dark Purbeck marble. Although the superb proportions and harmonious design of the cathedral's interior will impress you, perhaps you will not sense the same excitement as when you studied its exceptional exterior.

Turn to your right on entering the cathedral to view the great **west window.** It contains some of the finest and oldest glass in the cathedral, much of it thirteenth century. Stop on the right of the door to see the **clock,** made about 1386. It is believed to be the oldest working clock in England and perhaps in the world. As you wander down the **nave,** you will admire the graceful **arcades.** In the center of the cathedral directly below the spire you will find in the stone flooring a **brass tablet** indicating that the spire leans twenty-nine and a half inches to the southwest. Nearby you will note a pillar bent under the weight of the tower. There is a fine view of the nave and west window from the choir. Don't miss the interesting **inverted or scissor arches.**

At the east end of the cathedral have a look at the **Lady Chapel** with its thirteenth-century glass window.

In the transept opposite the choir you will find a great **cope chest** that dates from the thirteenth or fourteenth century and is still used. Look above you and you will see the American flag, a souvenir of the American troops stationed in the Salisbury area during World War II.

Turn left in the south transept past an interesting **alabaster tomb** on the left. The entrance to the fascinating **library** is through a doorway on the left just before you go out into the cloisters. Unfortunately the library is only open Monday and Friday 2:00–3:30. If you are lucky enough to be there at that time, be sure to visit it. Here you will see the most perfect of the four originals of **Magna Carta.** (The one with the actual signatures no longer exists.) Also on exhibit is the autographed survey of the cathedral by Sir Christopher Wren whose recommendations saved the spire. Other treasures are a remarkable **tenth-century psalter,** in old English, books from **William Caxton's** fifteenth-century press, a description and map of **Virginia** by Captain John Smith (printed in 1612), and **William Harvey's book** on the circulation of the blood (1628).

Stroll from the cathedral into the exquisite thirteenth-century **cloisters,** the largest and perhaps the most beautiful in England. Two tall magnificent cedars of Lebanon in the center of the lawn contribute to the monastic atmosphere. At the far corner, glance upward through the traceried arches for a fine view of the tower and spire.

Continue around the cloisters to the octagonal **Chapter House.** The vaulted roof springs from the central pillars in keeping with its late thirteenth-century style. Be sure to study the remarkable **thirteenth-century sculptures,** illustrating scenes from the Books of Genesis and Exodus, in the canopied arcading around the wall. These sculptured groups are among the most unusual of their kind to be seen in any Gothic cathedral.

On returning to the cathedral wander along the south aisle of the nave, stopping here and there to look at several interesting tombs. On your right is the reclining mailed figure of William

Longspée, one of the witnesses to Magna Carta and a founder of the cathedral. A bit farther along the **shrine of St. Osmund,** founder of the cathedral at Old Sarum, dates from the eleventh century. It is said that the cripples who prayed at the shrine placed their limbs in the openings. In a few feet you will see the fascinating eleventh-century figure of Bishop Roger, an early effigy. Just before you leave the cathedral, a memorial near the clock may interest you—the well-worn figure of Bishop Poore who founded the cathedral.

Cross the close for a better view of the great **west front.** A few minutes stroll to the left along **West Walk** will enable you to see the cathedral and spire from still another angle. On your way back along West Walk, you pass several charming Georgian houses, including the fourteenth-century **King's House,** now a teachers' training college. Just beyond it opposite the cathedral's west front is the **North Canonry.** Go under the arch of the old stone house. At the rear you will come to a magnificent **herbaceous border** that runs down to the banks of the Avon. This is indeed a peaceful spot made even more picturesque by the swans. The cathedral spire rising behind the delightful garden is a beautiful sight.

Back on the West Walk saunter past more attractive dark red brick houses with white windows set back behind flower-filled gardens to the circular green or choristers square. Here is the most elegant house of all, **Mompesson House.** Built in 1701, the interior of this exquisitely decorated and furnished home (open Wednesday and Saturday May–September, 2:30–6:00) is quite exceptional. The splendid paneling, lovely plaster work, and beautiful furniture make this home (which is still lived in) one of the most tasteful examples of an eighteenth-century house.

Turn left from the close and walk under the decorative stone arch leading into **High Street.** Old curio book and antique shops may tempt you. When you reach **Bridge Street** cross over and go right on the far side of **Silver Street.** Now look carefully for a sign "St. Thomas Church." Through a passageway on your left you will come into a small churchyard. **St. Thomas' Church,** founded in 1238, is largely of fifteenth-century construction. Its nave has an extremely fine **Tudor roof.** The great **fresco** above the chancel arch is quite an unusual fifteenth-century painting of the Last Judgment.

Returning to Silver Street, go left in a few yards on **Minster Street.** You will see on your right the six-hundred-year-old **Poultry Cross** shaped like a crown. Just a few doors further on Minster Street will bring you to the **Haunch of Venison Inn,** Salisbury's best restaurant, where you dine in the old timbered rooms of a building that is believed to be fourteenth century. About seventy-five yards will bring you to the **Market Square** on your right. (Market days are Tuesday and Saturday.) Cross to the far side, turn left on **Endless Street** past the bus station, then go right into **Salt Lane.** In about fifty yards on your left you will come to the **Pheasant Inn,** an attractive old pub where you can have a light lunch of sandwiches and salads. The stucco and timbered Tudor-style house dates from 1445. Coffee and brass utensils on the walls, as well as pewter mugs and measures, give the bar an attractive air. Ask the proprietor to show you the interesting shoemakers' oak-timbered **Guildhall** upstairs. For over four hundred years the Salisbury shoemakers guild has been meeting here.

Return along Salt Lane to Endless Street which runs into **Queen Street.** Number 8 is one of Salisbury's fine old buildings, the **"House of John A' Port."** This early fifteenth-century half-timbered house now is a shop specializing in pottery, china, and glass. Go upstairs to see the decorative seventeenth-century paneling in the front room. In the other rooms you will find paneling taken from old ships.

Continue along Queen Street and cross Milford Street. Queen Street now changes its name to **Catherine Street** and then to **St. John Street.** After passing the **White Hart Hotel,** perhaps Salisbury's best, you come to the **King's Arms Inn,** a half-timbered building that is probably Salisbury's oldest inn and may date to shortly after the cathedral was built. You may want to stop for a bitter in its attractive old bar.

Cross St. John's Street and return through the arch to the

precinct of the cathedral along **North Walk** for a final view of the cathedral and close before starting your walk to Wilton at the corner of **Crane and High Streets,** which you reach through the High Street gateway from the close.

Turn left on Crane Street, cross the stone bridge, and go left on Mill Road to the **Queen Elizabeth Gardens,** an attractive public park. Keep to the left and cross the far footbridge from which there is a fine view of the cathedral spire. Stroll along the paved footpath through the meadows and in about five minutes or so you will reach a weir. The ancient flint and brick building is the **Old Mill** in **West Harnham.**

This fascinating inn, which bridges the **River Nadder** by three arches, may be a modified version of the building known to have been there in 1235. The muniments from Old Sarum Cathedral were stored here during the construction of Salisbury Cathedral. Ask the proprietor to show you the old millrace and the original beams and rafters upstairs. If you happen to be here at midday, stay for lunch in this charming place (lunch Monday–Thursday and Sunday, 12:00–2:00). The ancient ford, still in use, the mill-pond, the cattle grazing in the nearby fields, and the pointed cathedral spire rising in the distance make this scene just like a Constable painting.

About fifty yards from the Old Mill turn right on **Middle Street.** Where the road makes a sharp left, keep ahead on the footpath marked Bemerton. You will be walking along the willow-lined banks of the Nadder. To your right you may see the cathedral spire reflected in the water. The path continues over a little footbridge and along the meadows, and again the ever present spire looms above the fields to your right.

At the end of the path turn left along a paved road past thatched roof cottages. Shortly you will come to a tiny church on the lower road and then the road runs along the river.

Turn right at the main road and follow the high wall of Wilton Park to Route A30 where you bear left. In a few moments stop in to see the parish church of **Fogglestone St. Peter** with its double row of trimmed yew trees. Just a bit further you come to a roundabout where you turn left, cross the **River Wylye** and go past the village bowling green to the stately stone gateway of **Wilton House.**

The present Wilton House (open Tuesdays to Saturdays, also Bank Holidays April 1–September 30, 11:00–6:00; on Sundays in August and the first three Sundays in September, 2:00–6:00), home of the Earl of Pembroke, was built by Inigo Jones during the mid-seventeenth century to replace an older house destroyed by fire that stood on the site of an eighth-century priory. Wilton is one of the most notable country houses in England, not only because of its fine design, both exterior and interior, but also because of its historic past that predates the present building. It is said that Hans Holbein prepared designs for the pre-Jones house built in the early sixteenth century. The present **central tower** is all that remains of this structure. Queen Elizabeth I visited Wilton in 1574; Sir Philip Sidney wrote "Arcadia" while staying here; Ben Jonson, Edmund Spenser, and Christopher Marlowe were some of the literary figures who came here. According to tradition, Shakespeare and his theatrical company presented the first performance of either "Twelfth Night" or "As You Like It" at Wilton about 1601.

You will get a taste of the magnificent grounds on your way to the house from the gateway. The interior is, in effect, an unusually fine art gallery. The rooms are distinguished both for their classic proportions and their collection of historic and distinguished works of art and memorabilia. Although guides are available to show you around and explain the significance of the furnishings, a brief summary of the more outstanding rooms may be useful. The large **smoking room** on the ground floor contains a unique set of fifty-five "gouache" paintings of the Spanish riding school in Vienna. The suite of **state rooms** on the first floor are outstanding among English country houses. The great **double cube,** designed by Inigo Jones, and considered one of the best proportioned rooms in England, is most elaborately decorated with its painted ceiling and paneled walls on which hang some of Van Dyck's finest paintings. Chippendale settees and chairs are among the furnishings. The **single cube,** another Inigo Jones room, is equally distinguished in its decoration and works of art. In the **upper cloisters** showcases exhibit such interesting pieces as Napoleon's dispatch box from the Russian campaign of 1812 and a lock of Queen Elizabeth I's hair with a poem by Sir Philip Sidney.

After visiting the house, spend some time strolling around the beautiful park. Great cedars of Lebanon and copper beeches dominate the broad expanse of lawn. Lofty yews harmonize with the Italian gardens. The eighteenth-century Palladian bridge over the Nadder adds a fitting classical touch to the luxuriant trees that arch the stream and the peaceful hillside beyond. Opposite the entrance to the house a wide walk leads to a secluded rose garden. Wherever you wander in this natural yet superbly landscaped park, you will admire the original planning and the perfection of its maintenance.

Before leaving Wilton House, you can have tea or a snack near the entrance gate. Wilton is also the home of the **Royal Carpet Factory,** in existence for three hundred years (open Monday–Friday, 9:30–4:00 except 12:30–1:30).

Buses leave at frequent intervals from the village or near Wilton House for the fifteen-minute return trip to Salisbury.

ATHELHAMPTON

Dorset has become a place "you mustn't miss." It is relatively untouched by tourists; it has a special character of its own that has changed little with the times; it is a corner of southern England where Londoners keep a cottage hideaway and somehow feel more secluded than they would in popular weekend counties like Sussex. Even the people in Dorset are different. They are known for their independence, clannishness, ruggedness, and love of the soil. They speak with a dialect that bears marks of Saxon origin.

The County also is at the very heart of Thomas Hardy's **Wessex,** and most of that famous author's life was spent in the area. This great nineteenth-century poet and novelist was of old Dorset stock on both sides, and he was born and bred here. It was only natural, therefore, that the beautiful, yet brooding, countryside he knew best should be the setting for his many distinguished novels.

In touring southern England, you will cross Dorset enroute from Salisbury to Devon. If you only have a short time to spend on the way, why not do a walk near Dorchester, the heart of Dorset and the Hardy country? Dorchester itself, which Hardy called Casterbridge in his noted novel *The Mayor of Casterbridge,* is a pleasant though not particularly interesting town. However, in the local museum (open Monday–Saturday, 10:00–1:00, 2:00–5:00) you can see Hardy's study as it was when he worked in it. There is also an interesting archeological collection of prehistoric and Roman exhibits. Some were excavated from nearby Celtic **Maiden Castle** two miles south of Dorchester. This ancient **fortified town,** or "great camp," has survived since 2000 B.C., in almost perfect preservation. It is an astounding monu-

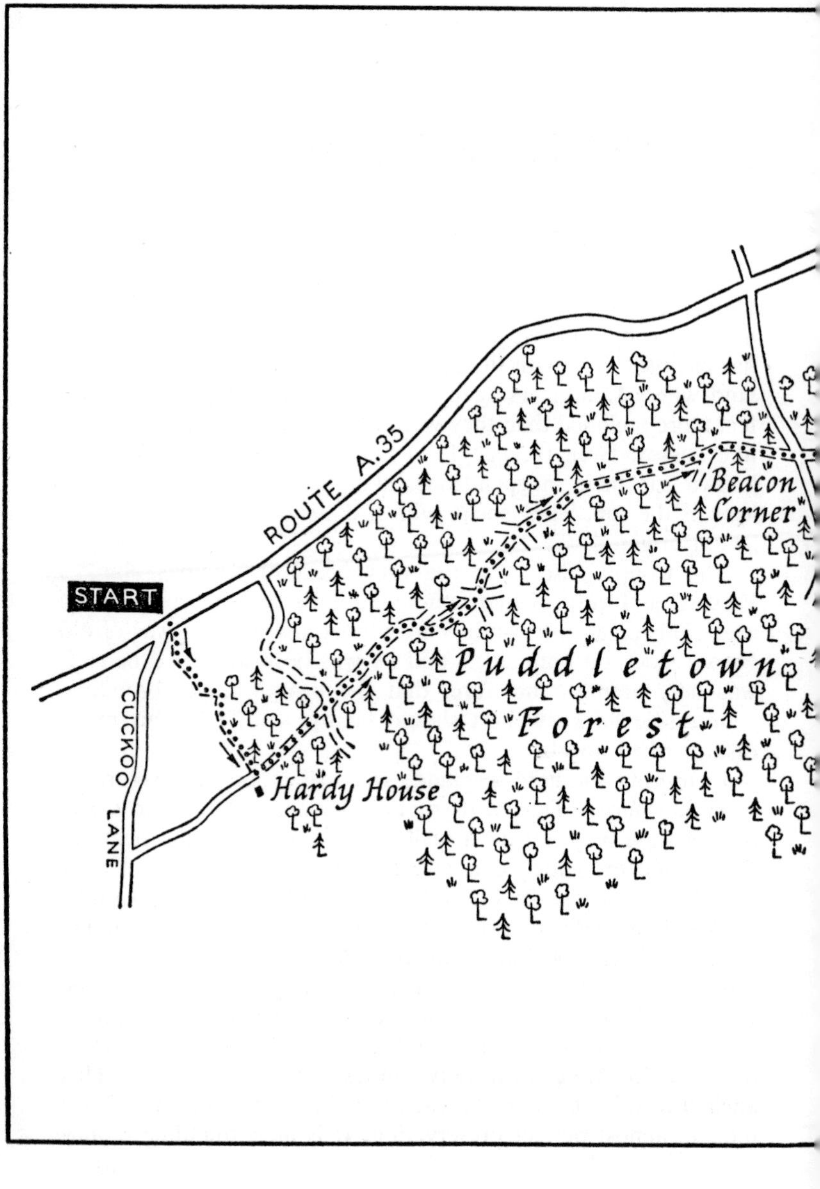
START
ROUTE A.35
CUCKOO LANE
Hardy House
Puddletown
Forest
Beacon
Corner

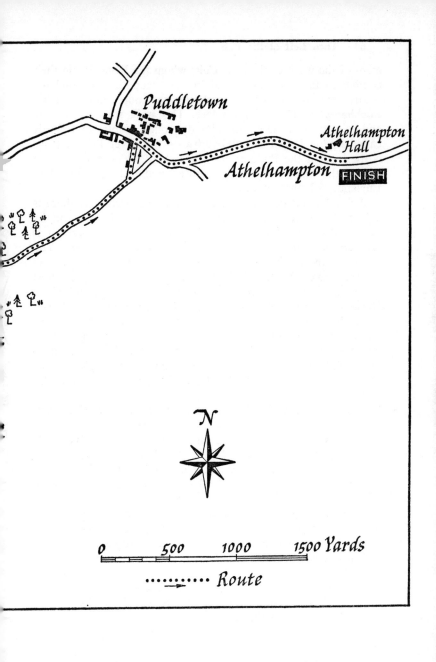

Puddletown

Athelhampton
Hall

Athelhampton FINISH

N

0   500   1000   1500 Yards

·········▶ Route

ment of the work of the busy Celts whom the Romans, on their coming to these shores, found in the occupation of England.

Just three miles east of Dorchester on Route A35 is **Higher Bockhampton,** Hardy's birthplace. This walk starts from here and goes through the moorland and wooded country that Hardy called **Egdon Heath** to **Puddletown** on the River Piddle. (This is the land of the Puddles and the Piddles.) You will finish at one of the finest and most beautiful medieval halls in all of England, Athelhampton.

If you should be traveling by bus from Dorchester, there is a half hourly service to Puddletown that will let you off by Higher Bockhampton turn at **Cuckoo Lane.** From here, it is about twenty minutes to the house where Hardy was born. You go up narrow Cuckoo Lane to the top of the hill where you can see the **Isle of Purbeck** in the distance. After passing the crest you take the first little road to the left and go to the end where **Hardy's cottage** stands on the right. Should you prefer a shorter route through the woods from the main road to the cottage, you enter an opening in the trees between two concrete posts about fifty yards to the left as you face Cuckoo Lane. Ten minutes uphill on this grassy footpath—one of Hardy's favorite walks especially in bluebell time—will take you right to his cottage.

If you are traveling by car, park at the corner of Cuckoo Lane and A35 and start the walk from here.

Hardy's cottage looks like those in storybooks. Its thick, thatched roof seems to envelop the low building while rambler roses entwine its small windows. The simple garden bursts with flowers and shrubs against a backdrop of beech, elm, and sycamores behind the house.

There is a feeling of seclusion about the cottage which fits in with Hardy's preference for a life rather "isolated from human contact where he could think uninterrupted."

Hardy described his birthplace in an early poem:

> It faces west, and round the back and sides,
> High beeches, bending, hang a veil of boughs
> And sweep the roof.

The rooms of the cottage (open Wednesday, Thursday, and Sunday, 2:00–6:00) are small with low ceilings. The modest furnishings are much as they were in Hardy's day. You will see many mementos of the novelist, including a set of his books. The cottage is well maintained by the National Trust and scholars of Thomas Hardy are encouraged to work here. If you are a Hardy devotee, you will find his birthplace fascinating.

You are likely to be shown around the cottage by the curator, Mr. J. P. Skilling. Hardy was born in the central upstairs room. He wrote two of his better-known works, *Under the Greenwood Tree* and *Far from the Madding Crowd,* at the window of his bedroom from which you get a delightful view of the garden.

Turn right from the cottage gate to start over **Puddletown Heath,** Hardy's Egdon Heath, which figures prominently in several of his books, especially *Tess of the D'Urbervilles,* his most famous novel.

Before you have gone a few yards from the cottage you will notice on your left a granite shaft erected in 1931 in memory of Thomas Hardy by "a few of his American admirers."

Go through a gate along the meandering grassy path on to the common or heath past clumps of low fir trees and wild rhododendron. As you cross the heather-covered heath towards the crest of the hill, the scene can best be described in Hardy's own words from *Tess of the D'Urbervilles:* "We went along the level roadway through the meads, and were backed in the extreme edge of the distance by the swarthy and abrupt slopes of Egdon Heath. On its summit stood clumps and stretches of fir-trees, whose notched tips appeared like battlemented towers crowning black-fronted castles of enchantment."

At the top of the hill several footpaths meet. Stroll about a hundred yards to the right to an open space in the furze for a good view over Dorchester. On returning to the crossing of the footpaths, bear left in the open heath and continue on the dirt road in the same general direction you have followed from the cottage. At the next crossing of the dirt roads, continue straight ahead and shortly you go down a slope, **Tolpuddle Hollow,** in the middle of the pine woods.

Soon you will come to **Beacon Corner.** Go straight ahead on the macadam road. In a few yards you will reach a magnificent beech grove. The boughs of these stately trees cover the road in such a lofty way that you have the sensation of walking through the nave of a cathedral. If you bear left at the road fork, you will shortly be in **Puddletown,** which Hardy called **Weatherbury** in *Far from the Madding Crowd.*

St. Mary's Church in Puddletown is well worth visiting. Built largely during the fifteenth century, the church has a beautiful **paneled ceiling** of Spanish chestnut, old oak pews of past days still in use, a Norman font, and interesting **memorial brasses.** The most picturesque corner of the church is the **south chapel,** or the "Athelhampton aisle," so-called because it is devoted to memorials to the Martin family, the ancient possessors of Athelhampton.

The chapel is justifiably called "one of the glories of Dorset." Its figures in alabaster and brass of the knights and ladies of Athelhampton are among the finest in all of England. Buried here are the Martins of many generations—the first of the race in 1250, the last, in 1595. Those who rest together here are men of one family and from one house, who, succeeding each other as father and son, ruled for nearly 400 years as squires in their little village kingdom. They lived through the reigns of sixteen English sovereigns—an impressive record in any day and age—and their effigies in the little chapel make an impressive old world story in stone.

No church in the county can compare with this one in human interest, and nowhere can one come into closer communion with the homely spirit of the Dorset of the past.

And now back to our walk—from the past, into the present, and then back into the past once more. From Puddletown, you can walk to Athelhampton in about fifteen minutes. However, you have to go on the main road. As there is no sidewalk, you may prefer to catch the bus, which goes every half hour from the **King's Arms.**

Even though **Athelhampton** is open officially only Wednesday and Thursday, 2:00–6:00 from Easter to September (also

Easter and Whitsun Sundays and bank holidays), you may be admitted on other days if you phone Puddletown 288 for an appointment.

Athelhampton is a remarkably well preserved fifteenth-century country house surrounded by superb gardens. It is not so large that it loses its charm and it is lived in which gives it the feeling of a magnificent home.

As you approach the house through the great gate, you will notice the fine **oriel window** to the left of the entrance court. The **great hall** on your left is the glory of the house and one of the finest in England. Its original open timber roof, beautiful linenfold paneling, and windows with panes of fifteenth-century glass in heraldic design give it a most distinguished air. Occasionally the Summer Music Society of Dorset presents a concert here—a perfect place to listen to classical music.

The **great chamber,** a most impressive room, faces the extensive lawn below which flows the little **River Piddle.** Directly above is the **long gallery** with a secret staircase leading to the floor below. Although the present furniture is not original, the furnishings of the house have been selected with great care to show the interior as it was centuries ago.

After touring the house, you should stroll about the lovely gardens. In addition to a fourteenth-century dovecote, there are, closer to the house, four well-landscaped **formal courts** enclosed by high clipped yews. Wander across the front lawn down to the River Piddle and then to the **thatched stables** on your way to the entrance gate.

To return to Higher Bockhampton, you can inquire at the house to find out what time the bus leaves which will let you off either at Cuckoo Lane (the route to Hardy's birthplace has been described above) or take you on to Dorchester.

SALCOMBE

In such a seafaring country as England where you are never more than seventy miles from the coast, you will want to take at least one walk along the shore. Though there are many attractive coastal resorts—particularly along the Channel—where you can stroll on the sands or walk along the cliffs, **Salcombe** in South Devon surpasses them all. You may think at first that South Devon is too far away unless you are touring Devon and Cornwall anyway, but once you have seen Salcombe you will agree that it is well worth a couple of hours drive or train trip from Dorset or Wiltshire.

Salcombe is located on a sheltered and wide estuary almost equidistant between Torquay on the east and Plymouth on the west. It is a popular fishing and sailing center—and the atmosphere of the village which nestles close to the harbor is as salty as its name. In Roman days salt was produced here by drying sea water in the nearby combes or valleys—hence Salcombe. Today there is a gay, nautical spirit about the wharves and boat yards along the inner harbor. In summer open skiffs, sailboats, motor cruisers, trim schooners, yawls, and luxurious yachts float at anchor just offshore.

There is a feeling of fun about the little narrow lanes and the amusing pubs perhaps because so many young people go to Salcombe in summer. Yet there is little gay night life.

Climate in England is a tricky matter—as every traveler to the island knows—but the South Devon coast is unusual. Salcombe's semitropical vegetation, palm trees, oleanders, and even banana trees (grown outdoors) testify to its balmy, mild weather compared to most English resorts. It has all the climatic advantages of Torquay—generally regarded as England's Nice—as

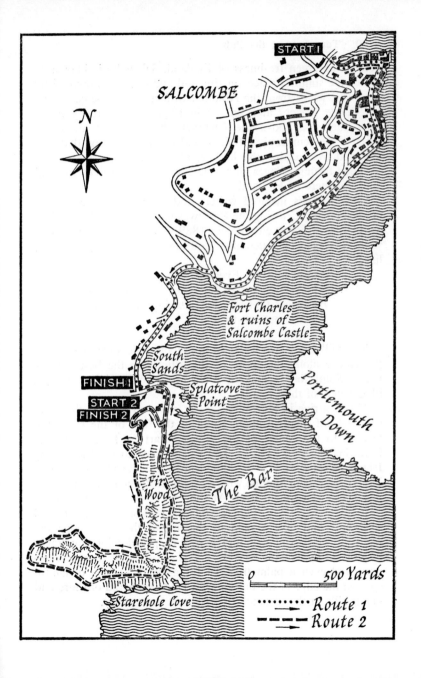

START 1

SALCOMBE

N

Fort Charles
& ruins of
Salcombe Castle

South Sands

FINISH 1

START 2

FINISH 2

Splatcove
Point

Portlemouth
Down

Fir
Wood

The Bar

Starehole Cove

0   500 Yards

•••••••• Route 1

━ ━ ━ Route 2

well as the green freshness of England. Salcombe is known as one of the sunniest places in England and usually is favored by southwest winds from the Atlantic. In fact, Salcombe can boast a veritable Riviera air—unique in England. The rocky headlands that rise above the Channel, the red cliffs along the estuary, the semitropical foliage and colorful gardens that line the road overlooking the harbor, all are more reminiscent of secluded fishing villages along the French Riviera than you will find elsewhere in England.

Salcombe has inspired writers and poets. Lord Tennyson's famous poem **"Crossing the Bar"** was written about the sandbar astride the estuary's entrance in 1889 while the poet was on the yacht Sunbeam off Salcombe. You may recall his often-quoted lines:

> Sunset and the Evening Star
> And one clear call for me
> And may there be no moaning of the bar
> When I put out to sea.

You will enjoy two walks in and about Salcombe—one from the village along the shore of the estuary to the best bathing beach, South Sands, and the other on the cliffs high above the blue waters of the Channel.

If you arrive in Salcombe by car, you can park in the main car park off **Shady Combe Road** at the foot of the steep hill leading to the center of the village. Start on foot from here following the sign "To the Town" and keep to your left along **Island Street** past boat-building yards. On the way stop in at **Ye Wrought Iron Shoppe** where Devon craftsmen make interesting pieces of wrought iron. At the end of the street turn right past Edgar Cove Ltd. (where you can rent sailing, motor, and rowboats) and take a path to the left of the road along the **sea wall.** Here you will find a row of pastel-colored cottages brightened by hanging baskets of fuchsia, rambler roses, geraniums, and even a palm tree not far away. This is a delightful spot on the edge of the harbor with boats anchored offshore and green hills in the distance rising above the estuary.

Go through the archway to **Union Street**—one of Salcombe's tiny streets. Over the archway is **The Loft Studio** with the exhibitions of paintings and art by members of the Art Club, open daily Easter to October. Wander into Offshore Ltd., an attractive shop selling a fashionable, international assortment of sportswear. Next to it at the corner of the quay is the **Salcombe Life Boat House.** In England lifeboats are owned and operated by the Royal National Lifeboat Institution, a voluntary organization financed by shipping companies and other private donors. You can usually see the motor lifeboat offshore. Just opposite stands Salcombe's **Custom House.** Seafaring, bearded sailors with their well-worn peaked caps are often wandering about the quay.

Retrace your steps along Union Street and visit **The Galley,** a waterside port of call for many people after a brisk sail or a day's sea bass or mackerel fishing. Turn left opposite the Fortescue past several little restaurants and shops selling pottery and pewter. Just across Clifton Place you come into **Fore Street,** Salcombe's main street. In a few yards glance down **Folly Lane** (only about four feet wide) for an interesting view of the harbor.

There's a car park on your left along the water's edge. On your right is the ancient **Victoria Inn,** one of the most delightful pubs in town. Stroll along the wharf to Powercraft's boat shed. Here, or at Powercraft's boathouse at South Sands, you can rent rowboats, outboard motor boats, ordinary and ocean-going sailboats. You can make arrangements for deep-sea and even shark fishing. On your way back to Fore Street, there is an interesting tablet on **Normandy Way,** commemorating the men of the U. S. Navy who sailed from Salcombe and "passed this way to embark for the Normandy beaches there to assault the enemy on D-Day, Tuesday the 6th of June 1944."

Continue along narrow Fore Street with its fascinating shops and crowd of gay summer visitors. Watch on your right for **Robinson Row**—a narrow lane lined with attractive cottages sporting bright flowers in window boxes. On the right as you go up the street, you will come to **Shipwrights Arms,** the headquarters of the Sea Anglers Association, where on the walls you will find pictures of the famous Salcombe Clippers of the 1840's to 1880's. You will pass the **Salcombe Hotel,** overlooking the harbor and perhaps the best in the town. Ask the hall porter to point out to you the **aloe tree** in the palm-filled garden. The aloe was planted in 1923 and didn't bloom until 1964.

You now are approaching **Ferry Corner** where the street becomes so narrow that it is only the width of one car. On your left a flight of steps leads down to the **Ferry Inn.** If you happen to be here at midday, go out in the garden overlooking the harbor and enjoy a light lunch from the buffet bar. While you are sitting in chairs made out of beer kegs and enjoying a sandwich and a half of bitter, watch the gulls diving for fish in the estuary. On the opposite shore you will notice the red color of the fields, characteristic of Devon's clay soil. Right below you is the dock from which motorboats operate a ferry service to South Sands and to Portlemouth across the estuary. Just above the Ferry Inn before you return to the main street, you will find the open-air **Salcombe Market Garden,** a charming little flower, fruit, and vegetable shop that also sells Devon's famous clotted cream.

You now walk along **Cliff Road**—a continuation of Fore Street. The **Salcombe Yacht Club** will be on your right and the recently renovated **Marine Hotel** on your left. There is a fine scale model of a Salcombe Clipper in the entrance hall of the Yacht Club. Keep left at the fork on **Undercliff Road.** Now you will pass fine houses with lovely gardens, planted with fine shrubs, palms, and great cedars of Lebanon. This narrow road, a couple of hundred feet above the water, runs between beautifully landscaped terraces. Here and there you have an uninterrupted view over the estuary, the beaches, and promontories on the opposite shore. In a few minutes you will see the ruins of **Fort Charles** or Salcombe Castle built by Henry VIII on a rocky crag offshore. During the Civil War this was the last Cavalier stronghold against the Roundheads.

After passing a new motel, you follow the road around the point and down the hill to a pleasant bathing beach, **North Sands.** Keep to the right beyond the beach and continue on the road to the left up rather a steep climb. Here magnificent beech woods line the road. You will discover a spot where, while rest-ing on the stone wall, you have a striking view through the trees towards the Channel. Also, the fragrance of pine trees is in the air. A few minutes' rather sharp descent along the typical Devonshire lane will bring you to **South Sands.** The **Tides Reach** on your right is quite a good hotel for lunch. For a simple meal, try the **South Sands Hotel** right on the water. South Sands itself is a delightful little beach—a good place to lie on the sand or perhaps have a swim. If you want to return to Salcombe, take the little ferry that leaves every half hour between 10:00 and 6:40 in summer from South Sands quay. Here you will notice the rise and fall of the tide—about fifteen feet between high and low tide.

The second walk starts at South Sands and will take you near **Bolt Head,** a noted promontory along the coast. You will stroll along the top and alongside the rocky cliffs that rise precipitously several hundred feet above the Channel. This is a dramatic and beautiful walk with marvelous views over the sea and can be done in about two hours or less. (Ladies should wear wide skirts or slacks and low-heeled shoes.)

You will have a steady climb up the road to the left from South Sands Hotel past the Bolt Head Hotel. Continue straight ahead on a footpath through a wood. Turn right, following the sign marked "Sharptor, Overbecks Gardens and Museum" at the fork of the path. **Overbecks,** a typical Victorian house, has quite an unusual **tropical garden** and a most amazing collection of Victorian oddities in the museum (open daily, 10:00–6:00; if door is closed, inquire at cottage opposite entrance gate). You approach the house by a drive lined with palm trees. Although you may be amused by the playing of the old fashioned polygraph and perhaps interested in the collection of curios, etc. in the house, the garden with its many semitropical plants, banana trees, and lovely flowers is worth seeing.

Continue from Overbecks on a path beside a stone wall, cross a stile marked "Bolt Head" and in a few yards turn left along a cleared path. Steep steps have been cut in the dirt path to make it easier to reach the top. Here you should pause and look around you for there is a spectacular view of the estuary, its wooded shores, indented bays, and Salcombe way in the distance.

Stroll along the top through a grassy field to the next stile. After crossing it, in a few moments **the Channel** spreads out before you–a sweeping view of the rocky headlands from Prawle Point to the estuary. Climb over some stone steps into the next field. At the end of the path you will be at **Sharptor**—above the crags and boulders—at an elevation of 429 feet above the sea. Look for the stone **sun dial** with a brass plate showing the direction and distance of Ushant, Eddystone Lighthouse, and the Channel Isles. Here you can rest on a bench and survey the rugged coastline.

From this point along the edge of the cliffs you should follow a footpath through the gorse and bracken. Shortly you cross another stile and just in front of a protruding rock wind your way down the slope through a field of bracken. You now are in **Starehole Valley,** once believed to be the site of a Danish encampment. Below you is **Starehole Cove.**

Presently you will come to the ruins of an old stone house. The path to the right goes on up the headland to Bolt Head for those who wish to extend the walk. Otherwise turn left along the footpath. Look above you at the jagged pinnacles of **Sharptor Rocks.** Here the path hugs the cliffs and is directly above the greenish blue sea. The drop is so precipitous that iron fencing and strong walling protect the path. Bolt Head is off to your right as you face the sea. A tiny island seems to be a nesting ground for seagulls. At this point in the walk you are likely to meet people who have strolled around the headland. On a warm summer's day you may encounter a tourist clad only in shorts and sandals.

In a few minutes the footpath goes around the point. **The bar,** which protects the harbor and which Tennyson made famous, lies below you—between the point and the opposite shore. At low tide waves break over the sandbar. On this part of the path you have a constant view of the estuary and Salcombe. Pause for a while on one of the frequent benches for a rest and more time to enjoy the scenery. When you resume your walk, go through a wooden gate and then through a wood where luxuriant trees overhang the path. After passing through another gate you will be out of the wood. Look over the wall and down below you will see **Stink Cove.** This last part of the tour from the point is known as the **Courtenay Walk.** From here you re-join the path where you turned for Overbecks. Continue down the hill to South Sands where you can take the ferry back to Salcombe.

WELLS

Wells is unique and completely captivating. It is the best preserved and least-changed cathedral town in England. At the foot of the **Mendip hills** in the heart of Somerset, Wells has retained its tranquil old-world character. A tiny place, its population is still only about 7,000. Here you will feel the atmosphere of an ancient medieval town. Since the cathedral was a secular foundation, Wells' clerical institutions suffered less destruction than other cathedral cities. The combination of the walled, self-sufficient ecclesiastical establishment and the small market town will give you a better idea of what a cathedral city must have been like several centuries ago than any other place in England.

Wells is a little more than half an hour's drive from Bath. Or if you are coming by frequent bus, it will take about an hour to do the twenty miles.

The town derives its name from the springs which rise very close to the cathedral and have threatened it throughout the centuries.

Begin your stroll (for Wells is so minute and full of one interesting place next to the other that you will stroll slowly) in the old **Market Place** with its **stone cross** and sixteenth-century **half-timbered buildings.** On market days vendors will be crying their wares from stalls where flowers, vegetables, and furniture will be on sale. There are several interesting shops around the square.

After looking about the market place, approach the **cathedral** through **Penniless Porch,** the carved stone gateway where beggars sat in former days. A few yards to your left in the close the marvelous sight of the magnificent **west front** of the cathedral will burst upon you.

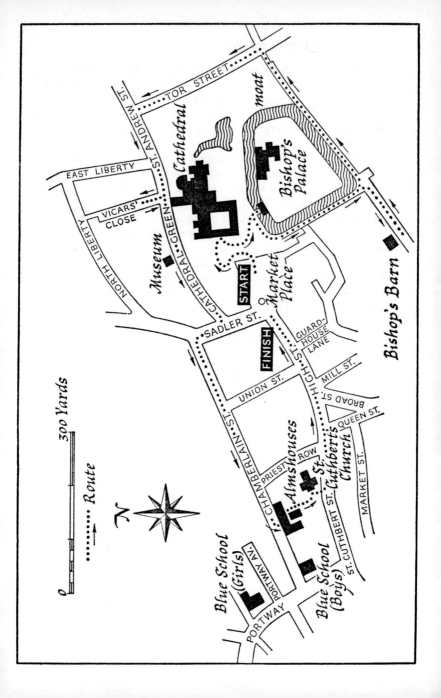

A church has stood near this site since King Ina of the West Saxons founded one about A.D. 704. The oldest part of the present cathedral dates from 1189 and the west front was consecrated in 1239. The cathedral with its central and western towers has stood very much as you see it today for almost five hundred years.

Before entering it, you should cross the lovely green to **Brown's Gate** for the best view of the cathedral's **facade.** The stone houses on your left are very old. (In the ancient gatehouse you will find a delightful tearoom with tables overlooking the green and cathedral—just the place for lunch.) Pause for a few moments by the gate to view the broad expanse of the west front and its two towers.

Cross the green to the brownish-gray stone front. It is heavily weathered because Wells Cathedral gets the full force of any storm from the Atlantic Ocean. There is no range of hills between the cathedral and the coast.

More than three hundred carved stone **statues** decorate this superb facade, which has often been compared to the cathedrals of Amiens and Rouen. This collection of figures is the finest group of medieval sculpture in the country. The front is unusual in another way for the entrance doors are quite small.

On entering the cathedral's **nave** with its graceful arches, the **inverted arch** beneath the central tower will at once catch your eye. These crossed arches were erected about 1330 to prevent the central tower from collapsing. Near these central archs are two beautiful stone chapels—the **Sugar and Bubwith chantries** erected in the fifteenth century. Another interesting **tomb** in the north transept is that of Bishop Still who wrote the popular children's poem, "Little Jack Horner."

The **clock** in the north transept is one of the cathedral's most interesting sights. Since it has a face, and Salisbury Cathedral's old clock does not, this is the oldest complete mechanical clock in England and dates from 1392. Be sure to see the clock strike the hour. Then the great bell on the tower strikes and the puppet figures of knights on horseback joust. On the quarter hour the figure of Jack Blandifer on the right sounds the note by kicking his heels and two jacks in fifteenth-century armor perform on the outside of the cathedral. The interior clock face is beautifully designed and decorated to show the days of the month and phases of the moon as well as the time. It is customary for visitors to join in reciting the Lord's Prayer after the clock strikes the hour.

Near the north transept you will find the wonderful **flight of stairs,** well worn during the centuries, leading to the **Chapter House.** Note the exquisite vaulting as you go up to the spacious octagonal room.

Stroll through the choir and look up at the great **east window,** dating from the early fourteenth century, in brilliant green and gold. While you are wandering about the nave and transepts, be sure to notice the beautifully carved **capitals** and captivating little figures chiseled in the stone, remarkable examples of fine medieval sculpture.

From the south transept you can enter the three-sided **cloisters.** Look through the arches for a fine view of the somewhat austere **southwest tower** which you can see from here independently of the west front.

A doorway from the cloister opens into the grounds of the **Bishop's Palace.** Stroll towards the **moat** which runs around it. The deep color of a great copper beech contrasts with the reddish sandstone walls of the palace. As you approach the gatehouse, you are likely to notice **swans** swimming about. They have acquired a habit, which seems to have been handed down from earlier generations of swans, of ringing a bell (which you will see below a window of the left gate tower) for more food after their daily feedings at 10:00 and 4:00.

The impressive brick palace dates from the thirteenth century and has been occupied by the Bishops of Bath and Wells ever since. The moat and battlemented wall were added a century later. Unfortunately the grounds are only open on Wednesday afternoons and some Saturday afternoons in summer. But if you stand on the inner side of the drawbridge you can see to your left the large courtyard, the ruins of the Great Hall, and the battlemented towers.

In the lovely **garden** of the palace there is a small pond fed by the seven deep springs or wells which give the town its name. The view of the cathedral's central tower rising above the lovely shrubbery and trees along the edge of the pond is one of the most beautiful in the close.

Turn left as you leave the drawbridge and wander past hawthorn trees along the wide **moat**—one of the most delightful walks in Wells. Now and again the cathedral tower is visible between the trees and above the **crenellated walls** that surround the Bishop's Palace. Here you sense a tranquil air of the past that harmonizes with the old-world spirit of Wells.

At the end of the walk, turn right along the recreation ground for a look at the ancient **Bishop's Barn,** a fifteenth-century stone building.

Follow the moat around the palace until you come to **Tor Street,** then turn left to **St. Andrew Street.** The back of the cathedral looms to your left. In a few moments you will pass **East Liberty,** a street on your right. The Liberty was the area that was at one time under the sole control of the Dean and Chapter of the cathedral.

Just before you reach the stone archway, turn right into one of Wells' unique spots—**Vicars' Close,** reputed to be the most complete ancient street in Europe. Built in the fourteenth century, the street and its uniform stone houses belong to the vicars of the cathedral. It remains substantially as it has been for six hundred years. Stroll along this row of houses with their tall chimneys and beautifully tended gardens. You will be enchanted by the little lawns and profusion of flowers—roses, fuchsia, hydrangea, and lavender. Notice how the close climbs to give an illusion of greater length. After walking to the lovely **chapel** at the end, return to the fourteenth-century **Vicars' Hall** and the **chain gate.**

On the other side of the arch, you will see the great face of the cathedral clock on your left. The **Wells Museum** (open daily, 10:00–7:00 and 2:00–5:30 Sunday July, August, September; 2:00–4:30 October 15–May 15), on your right, contains prehistoric and Iron Age relics of the nearby caves, Roman remains, natural history and other specimens. Just beyond it on your right, **the Deanery** is a fine fifteenth-century building. Wander into the courtyard for an unusual view of the cathedral.

Continue along **Cathedral Green** to Brown's Gate. On the way you will pass a delightful garden at a vine-covered and turreted stone house, No. 6. Part of this canonical dwelling dates back to the thirteenth century. Go through the archway and past the ancient gatehouse whose recorded history goes back to 1580.

Turn right on **Sadler Street** past old buildings, then left on Chamberlain Street. In two blocks after crossing Priest Row, you will reach Wells' unspoiled **almshouses.** The largest was founded by Bishop Bubwith five hundred years ago and includes the old city **guildhall.**

From the rear of the almshouses, where a few old couples still reside, you can reach **St. Cuthbert's parish church,** the largest in Somerset. King Alfred established the original church on this site in the ninth century and dedicated it to his patron Saint Cuthbert. Its square pinnacled tower, built in the early fifteenth century, in the Perpendicular style, and its sixteenth-century wooden roof, elaborately decorated with shields and bosses, are two of its outstanding features.

Turn left from the church on St. Cuthbert Street and stroll back along **High Street** past the old **King's Head Hotel** to the Market Place. Stop at the inn to see the fourteenth-century-old **monks' refectory** with its original rafters and beams. You will enjoy poking about Wells' byways and corners where old buildings have been modernized while preserving their ancient character. In a few moments you will be back in the market place where you may want to browse in the atmosphere of ancient Wells—an untouched treasure of medieval England.

BATH I

The elegance of eighteenth-century England comes to life in the historic city of Bath. The symmetry of its architecture, the grace of its crescents, the striking beauty of its Abbey, and its fascinating Roman remains give Bath a unique appeal. This eighteenth-century air, so prevalent in its squares and circuses, corners and byways, has been little touched by the realities of the present day. Bath retains that old-fashioned quality of living seldom found in English cities of its size. The pressure of modern industrial civilization, so evident in the streets of Oxford or Winchester, apparently hasn't left its mark on Bath. Perhaps the exceptional civic planning carried out by Ralph Allen and John Wood Senior and Junior in the eighteenth century has preserved the spirit of the days when Beau Nash established Bath's reputation as a social center and health resort.

The healing powers of Bath's hot mineral springs were possibly known to the ancient Britons. It was the Romans, however, so skilled in the use of health baths, who developed the only hot springs in the British Isles on a grand scale. They called Bath "Aquae Sulis" and the bathing establishment they built is one of the most complete remains of the Roman occupation of Britain. After their departure Bath did not again become a great health resort until the reign of Queen Anne and Beau Nash when the city attracted England's fashionable and literary world.

You should include Bath in any tour of the west country. It is close to centers like Salisbury and the Cotswolds (about an hour by car). A fast Pullman train reaches Bath from London in an hour and thirty-five minutes. Each June Yehudi Menuhin directs a distinguished ten-day music festival in the Abbey and elsewhere in the city.

There is so much to see in **Bath** that two walks are suggested so that each can be completed in a morning or an afternoon.

Start your first walk at **North Parade Bridge** over the **River Avon.** Standing here you have a picturesque view along the river of **Pulteney Bridge,** the Italian-style bridge designed by Robert Adam and the gay **public gardens** just below on your left. Often you will see swans swimming in the stream below the weir.

At the corner of **Pierrepont Street** turn left and pause at No. 2 where Lord Nelson stayed while visiting Bath. Across the street there is a pillar-supported Georgian building, **Linley House** at No. 1. It was the home of Thomas Linley, a noted composer, whose daughter married Richard Brinsley Sheridan. A nurse-maid in Linley's employ was the beautiful Emma, later Lady Hamilton, and mistress of Lord Nelson.

Walk along **Pierrepont Place** and around the corner to the left a few yards to the old **Bath Theatre** (now a Masonic hall) on **Old Orchard Street.** Here Mrs. Siddons gave her famous performances of Sheridan's *School for Scandal* and *The Rivals.*

Returning to Pierrepont Street, turn left on the wide sidewalk of North Parade and wander down narrow **Lilliput Alley** past some of the city's oldest houses. The alley leads into a quaint square, known as **Abbey Green.** A huge plane tree shades the delightful green, which is surrounded by several antique shops. You will discover as you stroll about the city that Bath is a great antiques center, one of the most noted in the country. From Abbey Green stroll up **Church Street** (to the right of Lilliput Lane) to **Bath Abbey.**

An exquisite gem of cream-colored Bath stone, the Abbey is a cruciform church in Perpendicular style. Although the present building dates from 1499, a Christian church has stood here for over twelve hundred years. A Norman church, of which only a few bits remain, was destroyed by fire before the erection of the Abbey.

Stroll around to the right of the Abbey to the little square opposite the great **east window** so you can admire the beautiful stonework, the flying buttresses, and the pinnacled tower.

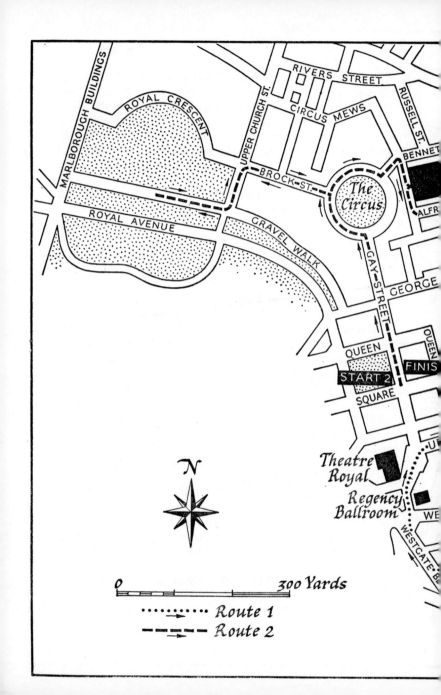

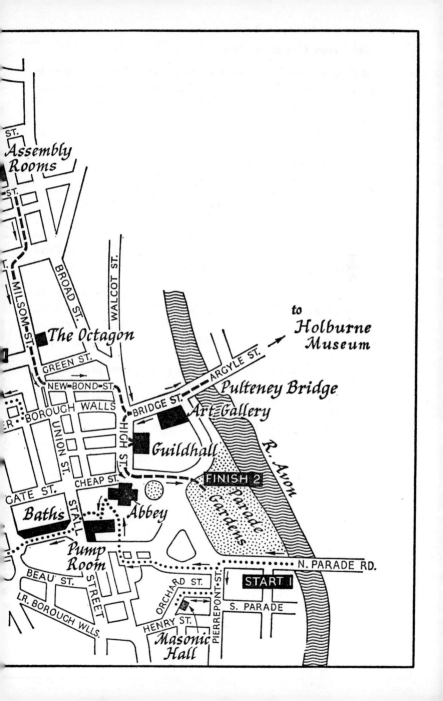

Before you go in the **west entrance,** stop for a moment to notice the remarkable carving on the west front—a representation of the founder's dream of saints and angels ascending and descending a ladder from heaven.

On entering the Abbey you will be struck by the magnificence of the roof **fan vaulting.** The great number of huge windows flood the Abbey with a brightness most unusual in English cathedrals. Though rather small in size, the Abbey has a grace and lovely atmosphere that is quite unmatched. Wander down the nave to the choir to see the new **East Window,** which replaced one bombed out during World War II. Don't miss the fine wrought-iron **grille** in the north transept, the superb **fan vaulting** in the north aisle or the richly carved **chantry of Prior Birde** on the south side of the sanctuary. If you are lucky, you may hear the excellent organ.

On leaving the west door, you will be in the Abbey **churchyard,** a large court. On your right you will find the City of Bath Information Bureau where you can obtain useful information about Bath and the surrounding country (open weekdays, 10:00–5:15; Saturdays, 10:00–12:00).

To your left is the entrance to the great **baths,** probably the oldest health establishment in the world (open 9:00–6:00; Sundays, 11:00–6:00 in summer; 9:00–5:00; Sundays 2:00–5:00 in winter).

Before touring the Roman baths, visit the **Pump Room,** a stately eighteenth-century assembly room. On your way into the spacious room, don't miss a charming print showing the scene at the time of Samuel Pepys. At the far end of the room a statue of Beau Nash stands above a clock, made for this room in 1709 by the most famous of all clockmakers, Thomas Tompion. You will admire the exquisite crystal chandelier and the eighteenth-century furniture. If you wish, you can drink the pure **mineral water** from a fountain in the Pump Room.

You should now descend to the **Roman baths** where the water gushes forth at the rate of half a million gallons a day at 120 degrees Fahrenheit. (It is worthwhile taking a guided tour.)

The remarkably preserved Great Roman Bath, open to the

sky, is the center of the establishment which the Romans used for three hundred and fifty years. The six-foot deep pool is eighty feet long and forty feet wide. The huge blocks of Bath stone around the pool and the diving stone date from the Roman period, as does much of the pool's lead lining. Parts of the lead conduit were laid by Roman plumbers two thousand years ago. There is an unusual view of Bath Abbey's tower from here. While touring the baths, notice the Roman system of underfloor heating. In a small antechamber you can see the source of the hot spring water.

You should visit the interesting **museum** to see a model of the Roman remains and also wonderful Roman relics. Two of the finest pieces are the pediment of the Sulis Minerva Temple and the beautiful gilded bronze head of the goddess. Other fascinating relics are the Roman memorial stones and a Roman curse engraved on lead, expressing a young man's frustration over losing a girl's favors.

After you have completed your visit to the baths, go through the **colonnades,** then turn left at a small square with a charming drinking fountain in the center. Stroll along **Bath Street,** one of the few streets in England colonnaded on both sides. Further along on your right is the physical treatment center where patients take the baths. At the foot of the street stands the medieval **Cross Bath** where Mary of Modena, James II's Queen, bathed.

Just ahead you pass through the **archway** of the old hospital of **St. John the Baptist** and go through **Chapel Court** to a street called **Westgate Buildings.** Turn right and in a few moments you will come to the **Theatre Royal** on your left.

The **Sedan Chair Restaurant,** just beyond the theatre, used to be the home of Bath's uncrowned king, Beau Nash, where he died in 1761. Cross opposite the restaurant and stroll along a street called **Upper Borough Walls** on the site of the medieval city wall.

Across from the Royal National Hospital for Rheumatic Diseases, which Beau Nash helped establish in 1742, turn into **Trim Street,** passing a charming little flower shop on your right. Before you reach the arch, called **Trim Bridge,** you will notice at No. 5 a large house with a decorative doorway on the right. General Wolfe, the hero of the Battle of Quebec during the French and Indian Wars, lived here in the mid-eighteenth century.

Beyond the arch you will be in picturesque, cobbled **Queen Street** with many small, quaint houses and little shops. This is one of the most attractive corners of Bath where you may want to wander about and browse.

At the top of Queen Street turn right into **Quiet Street.** The excellent antiques shop of John Kiel Ltd., considered probably the best in Bath and specialists in furniture, is on your right. The sight of lovely eighteenth-century pieces on display in Kiel's window may remind you of the days when this street was appropriately named.

Retrace your steps on Quiet Street and cross over to Wood Street. This will lead you to **Queen Square,** one of the most charming in the city. The classic and beautifully proportioned **north facade** designed by John Wood Senior is an excellent example of his distinguished architecture. His home was No. 24. While you are strolling around the square, which encircles a pleasant little park, it is interesting to recall that the novelist Jane Austen, who lived in Bath at various times during her life, resided at No. 13 in 1798. Two of Jane Austen's novels, *Persuasion* and *Northanger Abbey,* are connected with Bath and describe vividly life in Bath at the beginning of the nineteenth century. This charming square, with its literary associations, is a good place to end this first walk through Bath.

BATH II

This second walk through Bath will take you to most of those delightful architectural masterpieces that make the city such a fine example of the best eighteenth-century taste in civic planning.

At the northeast corner of Queen Square cross over to **No. 41 Gay Street** on the corner of **Old King Street.** This was the home of John Wood the Younger who carried on the magnificent classical building of his father. From the street you can see the small powder room. In its decorative recess the gentlemen and ladies of the period used to powder their wigs.

Continue along Gay Street past stone houses blackened with soot to **George Street,** the next on your right. About fifty yards on the left-hand side is the **Hole in the Wall,** the finest and most attractive restaurant in Bath and one of the best in the west of England. The proprietor takes unusual pains to provide first-class continental cuisine at a reasonable price so you should, if possible, lunch or dine here.

Proceed a few yards further along Gay Street to **the Circus.** The uniform beauty of this superb group of three-story houses that encircles the central green shaded by four plane trees is quite exceptional. Designed by John Wood the Elder and begun in 1754, these fine Palladian-style homes, with extensive gardens at the back, have recently been refaced. The Circus was so laid out that there is a true crescent between each of the three streets which lead off from it. Note the crowning acorns and the frieze that runs along the top of the entire circular group. Many distinguished people lived in the Circus—Lord Clive at No. 14, Major André (of the American Revolutionary War) at No. 22, and Thomas Gainsborough at No. 24. Today many of these fine homes are doctors' offices. As you leave, it is amusing to note the TV aerials on top of these classic houses.

Bear left into **Brock Street** and at the end turn left into one of Bath's lovely parks. As you stroll along, you will see the gardens of the houses you have just passed and the beautifully planted flower beds in the park.

Turning right into the gravel walk beyond the green lawn, there is the magnificent sweep of **Royal Crescent,** often called "the finest crescent in Europe." The sheer expanse of this dramatic architectural masterpiece is in itself overwhelming. Built between 1767 and 1775, these thirty houses constitute a noble ellipse over six hundred feet long. One hundred and fourteen tall Ionic columns support one continuous cornice designed in the monumental Palladian style. Pause for a while on one of the park benches to rest and to absorb this stupendous architectural effect.

Returning to **Brock Street** (unless you want to have a close look at the houses in Royal Crescent), turn left in a few yards along a passageway called **Margaret's Buildings** lined with small shops.

When you are back in the Circus, bear left on **Bennett Street** and take a sharp right to the **Bath Assembly Rooms.** This is another architectural triumph of John Wood the Younger. Bombed out during World War II, the beautiful ballroom, with its lovely high plaster ceiling, has now been restored to its original splendor. The five exquisite chandeliers are pre-Waterford glass and were made in London about 1771. (Open weekdays, 9:30–6:00; Sundays, 11:00–6:00 in summer; weekdays, 10:00–5:00; Sundays, 2:00–5:00 in winter.) Be sure to visit downstairs the intensely interesting **Museum of Costume.** Its collection includes fashionable men's and women's clothing from the days of Beau Nash to the present. Many of the costumes are shown against a background of Bath. You may be fascinated by one room completely filled with undergarments worn by ladies between 1815 and 1955.

Turn left from the Assembly Rooms into **Alfred Street.** The first large house (**Alfred House**) has a pair of iron torch snuffers on either side of the front door. Note also the pulley on the left of the door which was added in the days of Queen Victoria for the purpose of raising beer barrels at the time the house was occupied by resident employees of an adjoining department store.

From Alfred Street go right into **Bartlett Street** where you will find several antique shops. At the bottom cross over and stroll along **Milsom Street,** Bath's distinguished shopping street. (Most shops close Thursday afternoon.) Look carefully on the left for the entrance to **the Octagon,** an elegant eighteenth-century hall, originally a chapel. Its fine wrought-iron gates and handsome chandelier are well worth seeing. This part of town is a center of antique, silver, and curio shops.

At the end of Milsom Street cross over into **Old Bond Street,** about a hundred yards long and only for pedestrians. After browsing a bit in the attractive old shops here, turn into **New Bond Street.** D. and B. Dickinson on the left is well known for silverware. Glance down **New Bond Street Place** to your right.

If you happen to be at the end of New Bond Street around the middle of the day or late in the afternoon, go left for a few yards to visit the **Saracen's Head,** Bath's most ancient pub where Charles Dickens stayed while preparing *Pickwick Papers.* (It is right by the church.)

From the Saracen's Head, stroll through the **inn yard** and turn right towards the **Abbey.** Go left at Bridge Street and in a few moments you will be at **Pulteney Bridge,** one of Europe's few bridges (like Florence's Ponte Vecchio) that is lined with shops. If you have the time, continue along **Great Pulteney Street,** a wide avenue with fine homes. At the end of the street, beyond **Laura Place,** you will see the **Holburne of Menstrie Museum** (open weekdays, 11:00–1:00; 2:00–5:00; closed Wednesdays; Sundays, 2:00–5:00 and 4:00 in winter). This museum houses a collection of paintings, silver, porcelain, and pottery.

From Pulteney Bridge return along Bridge Street and go left on **High Street.** Here on your left is the **Bath City Market**—a lively spot where, under arcades, you will find stalls and shops selling everything from meat, flowers, and vegetables to curios, furniture, china, and glass. After wandering about this busy place, go into the **Guildhall** right next door on High Street. The upstairs **Banqueting Room,** elaborately decorated in the Adam style with a beautiful stucco ceiling, ornamental frieze, and eighteenth-century pre-Waterford glass chandeliers, is a magnificent hall (open Monday–Friday).

Turn left from the Guildhall, cross over behind the Abbey, and go into the **Parade Gardens.** Here, along the river, you can sit on the lawn in a deck chair, look up at Bath Abbey, admire the lines of Pulteney Bridge, or enjoy the beautifully planted gardens. It is just the place, over a cup of tea, to relax and recall the many charms of eighteenth-century Bath.

OXFORD I

Oxford and its ancient colleges is incomparable. The college towers, quads, cloisters, chapels, halls, and gardens—throbbing with life in term time and quiet as a monastery during the "vac" —will thoroughly excite you.

Though the city of Oxford teems with shoppers and is jammed with traffic, once inside the college gates the hubbub of the town disappears and at once the tradition of the centuries-old learning, scholarship, architecture, and history is all-pervasive.

There is much to see in Oxford, so three walks to the most interesting colleges are recommended. The walks appear in the order of their importance. This will enable you to fit your program to the amount of time you can spend and also will discourage you from cramming too much into one walk.

Oxford is easily reached from London—either just over an hour by fast train from Paddington or about an hour and three-quarters by car from Hyde Park Corner.

Start your stroll through England's Senior University in the center of the University, on **Broad Street** (or, as it's called in Oxford, "the Broad") at the corner of **Catte Street.** Though the colleges in effect comprise the University, this is the university's administrative headquarters.

Pause for a moment on "the Broad" by the weather-worn stone busts of the so-called **Roman emperors.** The classic **Clarendon building** on the corner was built by Hawksmoor in 1713.

Go up the steps and glance through the beautiful wrought-iron gates under the archway to the series of Bodleian arches and the Radcliffe Camera.

A turn to the right will bring you to the **Sheldonian Theatre,**

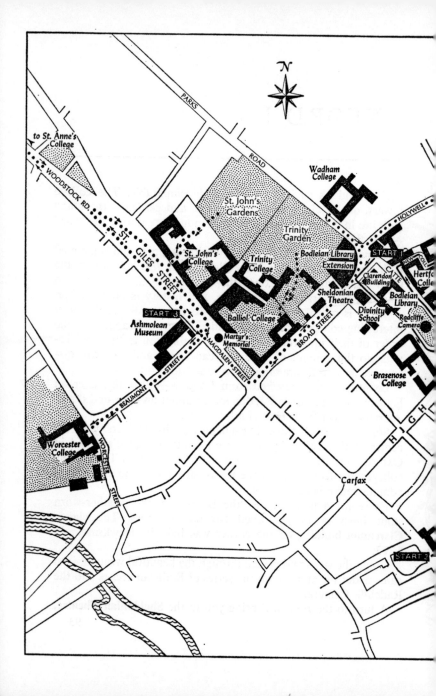

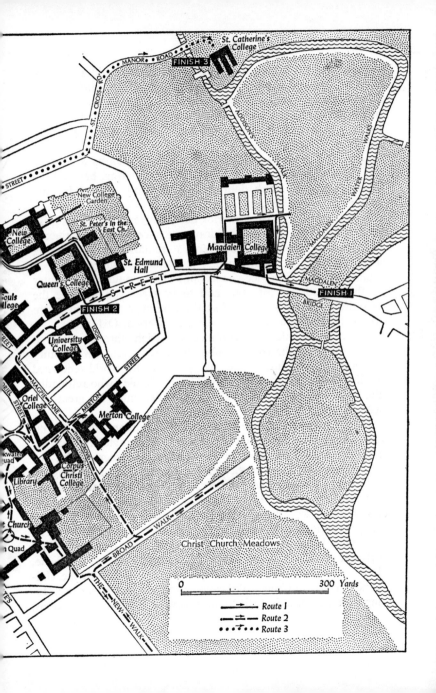

one of Oxford's architectural treasures. It was built in 1664–1669 to provide a place for university functions such as the awarding of degrees previously held in St. Mary's Church. Some of the ceremonies in the mid-seventeenth century had become too uproarious for a church, so Archbishop Sheldon provided the funds for a lay building.

Sir Christopher Wren designed the Sheldonian as a copy of the Theatre of Marcellus in Rome. Before entering, have a look at the huge oak **south doors** which are only opened for the academic processions.

The bright, impressive interior has been repainted in its original colors. Your eye will be drawn at once to the magnificent unsupported roof, one of Wren's remarkable engineering achievements. The painted ceiling is intended to suggest an open Roman theatre. The vice-chancellor's chair stands in the center of the curved tiers of seats and to its right you will see the beautifully carved rostrum. Ask the caretaker to let you go up to the cupola for a fine view over the towers of Oxford.

From the Sheldonian's entrance, turn right through the arch to the square of the **Old Schools.** This early seventeenth-century quadrangle now houses the old part of the world-renowned **Bodleian Library,** named for Sir Thomas Bodley who refounded the university library in 1602 when he presented his great collection.

The **Tower of the Five Orders** (Doric, Tuscan, Ionic, Corinthian, and Composite) dominates the quadrangle. As you go into the library entrance in the southwest corner, notice the sign above the doorway, Schola Medicinae, one of the original subjects of the old schools or lecture rooms. Go upstairs to see the fifteenth-century **Duke Humphrey's Library** and exhibition room (open weekdays, 9:30–5:00). Superb illuminated manuscripts, antique folios, and early records are on display. The seventeenth-century shelves contain books still arranged in their original classification by size and subject (Theology, Medicine, Law, and Arts). The elaborate ceiling, decorated with the University arms, and huge oak beams, give the room an air in keeping with the library's distinction. Following Bodley's instructions, a bell is still rung on the opening and closing of the library. Upstairs are reading rooms with decorative ceilings, painted panels, and quaint friezes.

On returning to the quadrangle, pass through the west door and a vaulted vestibule to the **Divinity School,** below Duke Humphrey's Library (open weekdays, 9:00–5:00, Saturdays, 10:00–1:00). Built in fifteenth-century Perpendicular Gothic-style, this room with its superb **vaulted ceiling** and great bosses is of exceptional beauty and nobility. The west door of the Divinity School leads to **Convocation House** where the governing assemblies of the University meet and where Parliament gathered when the plague forced it to evacuate London during the mid-seventeenth century.

Stroll through the central archway from the Old Schools quadrangle to the adjacent **Radcliffe Camera.** This circular building with a great dome and striking parapet, used as one of the Bodleian's main reading rooms, is a handsome eighteenth-century structure and one of Oxford's landmarks.

A few yards on your right as you face the entrance to the Radcliffe Camera is the massive gate tower to **Brasenose College,** known to Oxonians as B.N.C. (open 9:00 to dusk). Its odd name comes from the brazen doorknocker (a lion's head) of the old hall which hangs on the front gate. Stroll around the front quad to see the **Hall,** where another brazen nose is mounted above the high table. If you would like to see how a well-designed modern building can be crammed into small space behind the old quads, ask to see the new building put up in 1959–1961. A stone **statue** by Henry Moore stands nearby in the garden.

All Souls College (open 2:00–5:00) faces Brasenose on the opposite side of the Radcliffe Camera. Founded in 1437 by Archbishop Chichele, one-time owner of Scotney Castle, as a memorial to the soldiers in the Hundred Years War, All Souls has always been confined to graduate Fellows. For years an All Souls Fellowship has been considered one of the greatest academic distinctions available to nonscientists. Ask the porter at the gate for permission to enter the lofty and stately **Codrington**

Law Library, a stupendous room. Over the entrance you will see Wren's large **sundial.** Hawksmoor's **twin towers** with their pinnacles are prominent features of the Oxford scene. The wrought-iron **gates** facing Catte Street are particularly fine. You should also see the fifteenth-century **chapel** in the front quad on your way out.

On leaving All Souls, turn right on Catte Street and, after passing the Radcliffe Camera, go right underneath the bridge of Hertford College, **"The Bridge of Sighs,"** into New College Lane past blackened fourteenth-century stone walls.

The buildings and grounds of **New College** (open Monday–Friday, 2:00–5:00; Saturday and Sunday, 12:00–6:00; in vacation periods, 11:00–6:00), founded by William of Wykeham, are among the most enchanting in Oxford. The original foundation was called St. Mary College of Winchester in Oxford and the name New College may have originated to distinguish it from the older "House of Blessed Mary the Virgin in Oxford," known as Oriel. New College was the first college established for the sole purpose of preparing undergraduates for the arts degree.

After passing through the entrance gate, turn sharply to the left in the front quad. In a moment you will be in the glorious **cloisters.** Here more than anywhere else in Oxford you will sense the contemplative spirit of the Middle Ages. Stroll for a few minutes under the wood vaulting of the fourteenth-century cloisters. As you pause by the venerable **ilex tree,** at the far edge of the velvetlike turf, look up at the crenellated **bell tower** above the weathered, gray stone roof of the cloister. This is indeed one of the most tranquil and timeless spots in Oxford.

New College Chapel is quite outstanding. The ante-chapel contains windows of fourteenth-century glass and Epstein's dramatic statue of Lazarus. Look for the founder's silver-gilt pastoral staff and the original misericord seats in the chapel itself, which was largely rebuilt during the nineteenth century.

New College Garden is one of the delights of Oxford. From the front quad proceed into the garden quad, then through the superb early eighteenth-century wrought-iron gates emblazoned with the college crest and motto "Manners Makyth Man." The

extensive garden is L-shaped and stretches off to the right beyond the tree-covered mound more than three hundred years
old. To your left the battlements and bastions of the original
medieval city wall provide an historic background for the luxurious herbaceous border. From the corner of the garden near the
wall to the left of the entrance gates, you have an unusual view
of **Magdalen Tower.**

Turn left from New College gate and walk along narrow
Queen's lane that twists between high stone walls. In a moment
you pass on your right the new Provost's Lodge of **The Queen's
College.** From the lane it presents a fortresslike appearance but
its simple architecture harmonizes with the surrounding buildings.

As you turn into the High after passing **St. Peter in-the-east**
and **St. Edmund Hall,** on your right is the famous view of **the
High**—the classic facade of Queen's and the broad curve of the
High with the tall spire of St. Mary's rising above the tower of
All Souls.

On your way up the steps of The Queen's College, pause for
a moment to view the **clock tower** outlined by the entrance archway against the background of the sky. (Open in term, 2:00–
5:00; in vacation 10:00–7:00). Founded in 1340 by Robert de
Eglesfield, chaplain to Queen Philippa, wife of Edward III,
Queen's as you see it today was rebuilt in the late seventeenth
and early eighteenth centuries. Nicholas Hawksmoor, an associ-
ate of Wren, was the chief architect of the splendid **front quad**
which is cloistered on three sides. Directly ahead as you stand
at the gate beyond the unbelievably smooth lawn stands the
palatial facade of the college hall on the left and chapel on the
right.

The architectural glory of Queen's is the magnificent **west
facade of the library,** one of the finest in Oxford. Go through
the front quad and turn left in the early eighteenth-century back
quad. The east front of the library with its tall windows is most
impressive. A few steps beyond the library entrance you can
see the superb west facade surmounted by a stone eagle, the
founder's emblem. (You might obtain permission from the col-

lege porter to enter the Provost's garden to enjoy a better view of the library's facade.)

Be sure to enter the **library** (if closed, also inquire of the porter at the gate) in order to visit the **upper library.** This exquisite room of excellent proportions with its high windows has a nobility and dignity that you will seldom see. Principally designed by Henry Aldrich, a follower of Wren, it was completed in 1692–1695. Its highly decorated white stucco **ceiling** is superb and the Grinling Gibbons **woodcarving** on the tall bookcases is exquisite in detail.

Wander along the walled passage next to the Provost's garden and turn left into the old **Nun's Garden,** a quiet corner of Oxford attractively planted with rose bushes and flowering trees. **Drawda Hall** facing the garden is an example of domestic architecture prevalent at the end of the seventeenth century. On your way out, stop in at the lofty **dining hall.** The porter at the gate may be able to let you see the college's fine collection of old silver, including the founder's drinking horn which has survived six hundred years. Queen's is the only college where a trumpet is blown in term time to announce dinner.

Turn left from Queen's down the High toward **Magdalen** (pronounced Maudlin) whose magnificent bell tower looms ahead. Enter the college (open weekdays, 2:00–5:00; Sundays, 10:00–5:00; July 1 to September 15, 10:00–7:00) through the gatehouse on the left.

On the left just inside the college grounds (which comprise 100 acres and are the largest in Oxford) you will see the picturesque early seventeenth-century **Grammar Hall.** On your way to the chapel to the right of the entrance you will notice an **open-air pulpit,** the only one surviving in England. From the chapel follow the passageway beneath the **Muniment Tower** to the cloisters. Note the vaulting under the tower. Go up the steps at the right-hand corner of the cloisters to the distinguished **dining hall.** Its marvelous linen-fold paneling, fine Jacobean screen, oriel window, and portraits of distinguished old members of the college, including a fine painting of Cardinal Wolsey, make the hall perhaps the most beautiful in Oxford. Note the woodcarving and Henry VIII's coat of arms over the high table.

While you stroll through **the cloisters,** don't miss the colorful crests of famous old members overhead. To your right beyond a herbaceous border you will reach a small stone bridge beneath which perch and pike, safe from the angler, are frequently fed by visitors.

If you have about half an hour, cross the bridge to **Addison's Walk,** named after the great essayist.

Although you are only a few hundred yards from the noisy High, usually packed with traffic, a stroll around Magdalen's **water meadow** will transport you into a rural atmosphere. This walk is particularly charming in late spring when the may and hawthorn bushes bloom, and fritillaries fill the end of the meadow. The meandering **Cherwell,** overhung with willows, flows around the meadow. At the end of the island you will come to a little **footbridge** almost hidden in rich foliage. Stop for a few minutes to watch the passing punts carrying gay undergraduates of both sexes.

On returning to the main college grounds, you pass Magdalen's classic **New Buildings,** erected in the eighteenth century despite their name. Just beyond is the college **deer park** under a grove of tall and leafy oaks, chestnuts, and elms, where a herd of about fifty deer, one for each Fellow, add a sporting touch to academic life.

After you leave the college, saunter to the left a few yards to a point just beyond **Magdalen Bridge** for a memorable vista —the graceful, slightly tapering bell tower with its lovely pinnacles soaring above the tree-lined banks of the Cherwell. This is the ideal spot to finish this walk through the heart of Oxford.

OXFORD II

Start this walk through the inimitable colleges of Oxford at the most majestic of all—**Christ Church,** known as "the House" from the Latin *Aedes Christi* or House of Christ (open all day). If you approach Christ Church from **Carfax,** the center of the city, the magnificent proportions of **Tom Tower** will become increasingly apparent. Before entering the great gate with its tremendous oak doors, pause for a few minutes across St. Aldate's in the street leading to Pembroke College so you can study Tom Tower.

Cardinal Wolsey, founder of Christ Church, completed the tower's massive base to the height of the flanking Tudor turrets. Then in 1681 Wren added the octagonal and pinnacled cupola with its Gothic ogee windows behind which hangs the huge bell, "Great Tom," cast in 1680 and weighing over six tons. When the hands of the tower clock show 9:05 each evening, the great bell booms 101 times, 100 for each of the original students plus one added in 1667. Today Christ Church has the largest number of students of all the colleges.

As you enter the **gateway** look above you to see the forty-eight coats of arms of prominent benefactors, including Henry VIII and Wolsey, which decorate the roof.

When you step into **Tom Quad,** you will be spellbound by its simple splendor. Cross the broad expanse of lawn to the stone terrace past the central pool with its statue of Mercury. You will notice that the arches and pillars built in the walls on the four sides of the quad indicate that Wolsey planned a cloister to encircle the court. From this point you can appreciate the grandeur of Tom Tower and its grandiose court. You may happen to be here when the quad is empty and a serene stillness accentuates its enormous scale.

Turn to your right as you face Tom Tower. At the corner of the quad you pass **the Deanery** and then go through an archway. In a few yards you will reach **Peckwater Quad,** an excellent example of the Palladian style. The magnificent **library** on your right, recently refaced, now has a delicate tawny coloring (open 2:30–4:30). It houses the finest collection of paintings owned by any Oxford college. The **Upper Library,** housing the collection of drawings, is a nobly proportioned room.

Returning to Tom Quad you should visit the **Cathedral,** Oxford's most beautiful church with one of the oldest spires in England, which you can see well from the gateway of Tom Quad. Several features of the cathedral will catch your attention—the twelfth-century Norman pillars, the lovely fifteenth-century choir vaulting and the double arches of the nave. In addition to the seventeenth-century vice-chancellor's throne and a Jacobean pulpit, there are several interesting old tombs and monuments. The small fifteenth-century cloisters are worth seeing.

When you return to Tom Quad, on your left stands the squat battlemented tower and pinnacled buttresses of the hall.

Before you go through the archway under this tower, turn back to view impressive Tom Quad from still another angle. Take your time going up the **Great Staircase** with its great lanterns so you can study the remarkable **fan tracery** in the roof, a superb example of stone craftsmanship. The **Great Hall** (open weekdays, 2:00–4:00) at the top of the wide stone staircase is Oxford's largest. The lofty hammerbeam oak roof is richly carved and gilded. Christ Church's interesting collection of portraits, the finest in any Oxford college hall, adorn the paneled walls. Reynolds, Gainsborough, Romney, and Lawrence are represented. In addition to Henry VIII, Elizabeth I, and Wolsey, noted subjects include John Locke, C. L. Dodgson ("Lewis Carroll"), a former canon of Christ Church, and William Penn, an old member.

You should visit the huge **college kitchen,** down a flight of stairs to your right as you leave the hall. It has been used since the days of Wolsey and is the oldest part of the building. The original oak roof is more than fifty feet high. You can see the old chopping block and a great elm serving table six to eight inches thick, made in 1734 and used for 210 years. The original spit is still operated on special occasions and the old copper skillets hanging on the walls are in regular use.

You should leave the college by going from the Great Staircase through several passageways to the archway of the **Meadow Buildings** that leads to the **Broad Walk** in **Christ Church Meadow.** If you can spare a half hour or so, you will enjoy strolling down the New Walk to the **River Isis** (the Thames or in Latin *Thamesis* and hence called in Oxford Isis). Stroll along the path by the gaily colored college barges. If it is term time, several of the college eights will be out on the river. Continue this circular walk by the tree-covered branches of the Cherwell (which flows into the Isis) and return to the Broad Walk, an avenue of fine trees.

Turn right along the path to **Merton Street** before you reach Christ Church. On your right there is a striking view of Magdalen Tower across the playing field. The solid **Tower of Merton** rises ahead and on its right you can see remains of the old city wall. On your left you pass the attractive **Fellows' Garden** of Christ Church.

Turn left on Merton Street and have a look at **Corpus Christi College** just a few yards on your left (open 2:00–4:00 in term and Christmas vacation; 10:00–6:00 in Easter and summer vacation). The fine sixteenth-century **sundial,** a copy of which is at Princeton University, dominates the front quadrangle. The **college library** is one of Oxford's most picturesque and the hall has an original hammerbeam roof. Above the gate tower there is an elaborately paneled room with plaster ceiling of the Tudor period and an oriel window.

From Corpus, pass the Doric gate of Christ Church and keep left into **Bear Lane.** In a few moments you will come to the tiny **Bear Inn.** One of Oxford's most attractive pubs, it dates from the thirteenth century. In the Bear's oak-beamed bar, with an extraordinary collection of three thousand club ties in cases around the walls, you can enjoy a snack or a drink.

If you pass here when the pubs are closed, don't go further than **Oriel Square** opposite the entrance to Christ Church. On your right is **Oriel College** which takes its name from a protruding oriel window. One of its best known members was Cecil Rhodes, founder of the Rhodes scholarships at Oxford.

Turn left into Merton Street and after passing the tower, go through the gateway into the grounds of **Merton College,** founded in 1264 (open 10:00–4:30). Despite the claims of University and Balliol, some consider Merton to be Oxford's oldest college.

Ask the porter to direct you to fourteenth-century **Mob Quad,** the most ancient quadrangle in Oxford. The medieval **library** (open 10:00–4:30) on the south and west sides is the oldest in England and one of the most fascinating rooms you will see anywhere. Built in 1373–1378, its high wooden oak bookcases, low paneled ceiling, and dormer windows give it an intimate air. This interesting relic of the Middle Ages still displays a few chained volumes to illustrate how books used to be protected from unauthorized borrowers.

From here you go through a passage to reach **Merton Chapel,** the first, largest, and certainly one of the most glorious in Oxford. The lofty crossing and vaulting in the chapel is one of its noblest features. The choir dates from 1290. Note its fine windows which contain unique painted glass of the same period. The tower above was completed in 1450.

Before you leave Merton, ask the porter at the gate if you can have a look at the college's lovely **garden** overlooking Christ Church meadow.

Turn left from Merton, cross the street and saunter along narrow **Magpie Lane.** Its odd little houses are quaint. The slender spire of **St. Mary's** looms at the High Street end. If you want a fine view over Oxford, you can climb St. Mary's ninety-five-foot tower (open weekdays, 10:00–5:00; Sunday, 1:00–5:00).

On reaching the High, turn right to the entrance of **University College,** one of Oxford's few thirteenth-century foundations.

Go through the seventeenth-century front quadrangle to the **chapel.** Its seventeenth-century painted glass windows are considered perhaps the best and most complete in Oxford. Note the fine carving of the screen. At the northwest corner of the front quad you will find the **Shelley memorial.** The sensitively modeled marble figure of the drowned poet, who was "sent down" in 1811 for his pamphlet "The Necessity of Atheism," is a moving piece of work. Ask the porter at the lodge to direct you to **Helen's Court,** a charmingly converted row of old almshouses. When you leave the college, turn right on the High for a few yards, then right again along **Logic Lane** to see the attractive modern quad of lecture and dormitory buildings given by Prof. A. L. Goodhart, the first American ever to be elected Master or head of an Oxford college.

Return along Logic Lane to the High. Here at its famous curve is the place to pause again before one of the most memorable vistas in Oxford—a fitting place to end this walk.

OXFORD III

Start this walk through the ever fascinating colleges of Oxford at the top of **St. Giles Street,** called the "Giler." Pause for a moment by the **Martyrs' Memorial,** erected to commemorate the Protestant reformers Latimer, Ridley, and Archbishop Cranmer who were burned at the stake in Broad Street during the reign of Catholic Queen Mary. A cross in the road marks this historic spot.

You will be impressed by the spaciousness of the wide street, which divides at the end into the Woodstock Road on the left and Banbury Road on the right. About five minutes up the **Woodstock Road** will bring you on the right to **St. Anne's College,** one of the women's colleges, which has recently erected a most striking modern dining hall with high glass windows.

Stroll back along the "Giler" to one of Oxford's most attractive colleges, **St. John's** (open weekdays, 9:00–5:00; Sunday, 10:00–1:00). Go through the fifteenth-century gatehouse into the front quad and continue into **Canterbury quad,** named for its builder William Laud, Archbishop of Canterbury. This splendid quadrangle is the most grandiose example of early seventeenth-century architecture in Oxford. When you enter the quad, at once you are struck by the graceful arches of the Italian colonnade, a combination of Gothic and classical styles.

St. John's garden is the largest and certainly one of the loveliest of any Oxford college. Stroll across the extensive lawn for a good view of the stately **east facade** of Canterbury quad. Magnificent copper beeches shade a delightful corner near the **rockery,** one of the oldest in England. As you poke about the rock garden or saunter by the deep herbaceous border, it's hard to realize that such a spacious haven of repose can be within hundreds of yards of the traffic-clogged and shopper-crowded Cornmarket, Oxford's main shopping street. On leaving this glorious garden, notice the shell paneling on the wooden entrance door.

St. John's Hexagon building, near the front quad, is also well worth seeing. Considered one of the best contemporary buildings in Oxford, its six-sided design of stone and glass is unusual and blends well with the earlier buildings in the courtyard. A huge elm in the center adds a softening touch to the buildings.

Cross "the Giler" and turn right at the corner of **Beaumont Street** to visit the recently renovated **Ashmolean Museum** (open weekdays, 10:00–4:00; Sundays, 2:00–4:00). The university's distinguished art and archeological collection is noted for a representative selection of European paintings, perhaps the finest outside of London. Its group of modern French art is outstanding and its collection of drawings by Michelangelo and Raphael exceptional. Among the museum's treasures are its Egyptian and Cretan antiquities, its unusual display of Chinese porcelain, and its great collection of seventeenth- and eighteenth-century silver.

Continue down Beaumont Street to **Worcester College,** which you will see ahead. From the gate walk through the loggia and turn left to the row of fine low buildings, the relatively untouched fifteenth-century **cottages.** Originally separate monastic houses, the ancient shields over the doorways indicate the different abbeys with which they were associated. Note the amazing medieval brickwork. Go through a narrow passage to the large **garden** with tall, luxuriant trees. Here you will find Oxford's only lake and the college's famous swans. From the garden you have a fine view of the aristocratic **Provost's Lodgings,** now occupied by Lord Franks, former British Ambassador to the United States.

Return past the regency houses of Beaumont Street, cross the "Giler" again and stroll along Broad Street to **Balliol** (open 2:00–5:00). Although its buildings verge on the hideous, Balliol is so distinguished academically that you should set foot on its grounds. The **garden quadrangle** is most attractive, with its irregular shape, fine lawns, and magnificent chestnut trees.

Leaving Balliol turn left and into **Trinity,** the adjoining college (open 2:00–7:00). The fine wrought-iron gates by the **Porter's Lodge** were made in the year of the American Revolution. Have a look at Trinity's seventeenth-century beautifully proportioned **chapel.** Inside you will see a magnificently carved screen and altarpiece attributed to Grinling Gibbons, as well as a richly decorated ceiling. Stroll into Trinity's extensive **garden** with its lime walk—a delightful place in spring when the flowering trees are in blossom. Wren designed the building at the north end— one of the first classical buildings in Oxford. On your way back to the gatehouse, note the row of picturesque **cottages** that face "the Broad" and the buildings in the background on your left.

Turn left on "the Broad" past **Blackwell's,** Oxford's famous bookshop and one of the most complete anywhere. Blackwell's tradition is that you are equally welcome whether you wish to buy or browse. On the corner of **Parks Road** stands the **Bodleian Library extension,** completed in 1940, which can hold five million volumes.

A few yards to your left along Parks Road will bring you to **Wadham College.** Just inside the big front quad you face the ornamental Jacobean **porch.** The doorway beneath leads to **the hall,** the third largest in Oxford and one of the finest, with its hammerbeam roof, Jacobean screen, and interesting portraits. Wander into the lovely **garden.** Its cedars of Lebanon, magnificent copper beeches, and gorgeous herbaceous border make it one of the most delightful you will see. When you look closely at the remarkable lawn, you are reminded of an Oxford gardener's remark. When asked how it is possible for grass to be so carpetlike, he replied: "First you roll it this way for a hundred years and then that way for another century." Before leaving Wadham have a look at the **new buildings,** erected in 1948–1953 and one of the most successful of the postwar construction in Oxford.

Turn left from Wadham and at the corner of **Holywell** turn left again. Walk along Holywell past some of Oxford's most attractive old houses and the buildings of New College. At the next corner, **St. Cross Road,** you turn left to visit Oxford's newest college, **St. Catherine's.** In a few minutes you bear right along **Manor Road** to enter the flat meadows surrounded by branches of the River Cherwell. Here the noted Danish architect, Arne Jacobsen, designed the complete set of college buildings—the most interesting example of modern architecture in Oxford. Two long symmetrical blocks of flat-roofed residential buildings of yellow brick enclose a large court with circular lawn. T-shaped common rooms and a fine dining hall occupy the north end of the site. Between the long three-storied block stands a 70-foot belfry above a high and spacious library. Its interior is most impressive. You will find it most interesting not only to wander around the courts of this brick and concrete college but also to examine the details of the hall, common rooms, and library. (Ask the college porter at the entrance for permission.) For example, the high table and tall-backed chairs in the dining hall are of most unusual and imaginative design. Note the marblelike concrete of the hall's thin roof beams. The entire college is so unlike any other Oxford college that you will find it a most interesting change. Opened in 1964, St. Catherine's, under its master Alan Bullock, has a larger proportion of undergraduates studying the sciences than is generally true in other Oxford colleges.

Here in Oxford's most modern college is the fitting place to end your tour of England's oldest university.

CHIPPING CAMPDEN

Any walking tour of the English countryside should certainly include—even if only for a weekend—a visit to **the Cotswolds.** Less than a hundred miles from London (about two and a half hours by car) the hills and vales of the Cotswolds have a unique appeal because of their famous and picturesque villages and the houses built out of Cotswold honey-colored limestone. This special stone is characteristic of the Cotswold country, not only for use in homes, barns, and farm buildings, but also for field walls and fences. The most artistic stonecraft is in the churches.

Two Cotswold small towns or large villages (depending on your point of view)—in many ways the most interesting, typical, and enchanting of all—are Chipping Campden and Broadway. Of the two, Broadway is the better known and consequently more crowded. But Chipping Campden is the more attractive, with more places of interest yet quieter and more distinguished. Each community clusters around a main street. Chipping Campden's main street has been called by G. M. Trevelyan "the most beautiful village street in England." Both lie at the foot of hills —Broadway on the edge of the **Vale of Evesham** below a steep hill and Chipping Campden snuggling between surrounding uplands.

They are close together—you can walk from Chipping Campden to Broadway in two hours or less. It's not a hard walk. By starting at Chipping Campden you descend the long hill into Broadway and you have only a slight climb on leaving Chipping Campden.

It is possible to reach Chipping Campden by bus from such railway centers as Moreton-in-the-Marsh (where the Manor

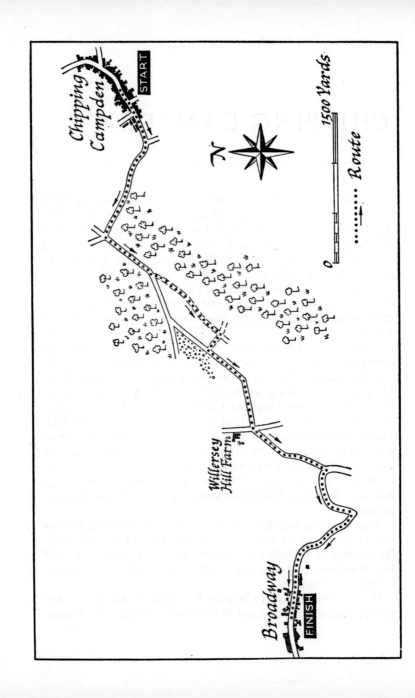

House Hotel, one of the best country hotels in all of England, is located). However, you probably will have a car for a Cotswold visit. After you have walked to Broadway, you can get a taxi in Broadway (opposite the Lygon Arms) to return to Chipping Campden for a reasonable fare of about $1.50.

Chipping Campden's name is a combination of Anglo-Saxon and Middle English. Chipping comes from the Middle English "Chyppen," to barter or market, and Campden is derived from the Anglo-Saxon "kamp" meaning "battle" and "deen" meaning "valley."

When you come into Chipping Campden you are at once struck by the rows of yellowish-gray stone houses that flank the broad **High Street** which curves so gracefully from the **Market Square.**

Start your walk here—there's a car park nearby. The seventeenth-century **Market Hall,** standing on an island in the High Street, is the architectural trademark of Chipping Campden and the town's most important building. Originally it was a market for perishable foods, not wool, despite the town's historic association with the wool trade. The ten semicircular **stone arches** of its arcade are surmounted by decorative gables. Pause for a moment and look past this artistic structure to the sweep of the High Street beyond. Aside from the beauty of the scene, you will sense the absence of commercialism. The little shops unobtrusively fit into the pattern of the harmonious yellowish stone buildings.

Before strolling up the High Street, note the two medieval cottages next to the Midland Bank near the Market Hall. It's amusing to see television aerials sticking up over the tiled roofs of these ancient buildings. **Rosemary Cottage** is particularly attractive with its garden and three mountain ash trees.

As you wander past the interesting houses towards the curve of the High Street, you will pass the **Grammar school** founded in 1487, now used for the headmaster's residence. The **Woolstaplers' Hall,** formerly a wool exchange during the fourteenth century, is another fine building of the period when Chipping

Campden was an important and prosperous center of the wool trade.

Farther along you take **Church Street** that bears to the right. Here on a raised terrace are the seventeenth-century **almshouses.** They were built in the shape of the letter "I" in honor of King James I. The view of the almshouses with the church tower in the background is one of Chipping Campden's most picturesque scenes.

A couple of minutes will bring you to the **parish church,** one of the finest in the Cotswolds. The magnificent 120-foot tower, with its slender pinnacles decorated with gilt weather vanes, dominates the fifteenth-century building. You approach the entrance beneath a stately **avenue of limes** planted in 1770. The church's interior is spacious and beautifully proportioned. In addition to its priceless medieval altar hangings, you should look for several **ornamental brasses.** The finest is that commemorating the death in 1401 of William Grevel, Chipping Campden's leading wool merchant and a contemporary of Chaucer's. Don't miss the wool-staplers' mark, the Globe and Pennon, nor the inscription to Grevel as "the Flower of the Wool Merchants of all England." In the **Hicks Chapel,** a memorial to Chipping Campden's seventeenth-century benefactor who built the Market Hall and almshouses, there are several sculptures, especially a fine bust of his daughter, Penelope.

Return to the High Street and cross over to see the impressive **Gothic house** that William Grevel built in 1390. The excellent condition of its two-storied bow window, five gables, and Gothic doorway make it one of the finest and best preserved fourteenth-century houses in England. Note the old **sundial** on one of the gables. From the front of the Grevel house you get a good view of the church tower.

Walk along this side of High Street, glancing down open gates to the gardens behind the houses. You may want to wander about some of the antiques shops. One has suits of mail, old powder horns, and various unusual curios. Look into the attractive courtyard with flowers and hanging baskets next to the **Noel Arms.** Should you wish to have lunch before starting off for

Broadway, there are several small inns and pleasant tearooms in the town.

If you feel like a short stroll before you start your walk to Broadway, turn into **Sheep Street** near the Market Hall. Down this street sheep used to be brought for shearing. In a few minutes you will come to several extremely attractive modern Cotswold stone houses with thatched roofs and gardens bursting with lovely flowers.

Begin your walk to **Broadway** at the west end of the town. You go down the lower end of High Street past a huge elm tree several hundred years old and the Roman Catholic Church.

Bear right at the road junction. Behind the iron gates you will see a fine house, **Westington Mill,** with a little stream running through the grounds. Go uphill on **Dyers' Lane** past the driveway to a fine house on your left. Just before you reach the top of the hill, turn around for a superb view of Chipping Campden's pointed roofs, little chimneys, and stone houses with their yellowish-tan color in the sunlight.

At the road intersection at the top of the hill you turn left (the sign points to Broadway) and shortly you will have another fine view of Chipping Campden nestling in the valley. From here the majestic church tower is clearly visible over the housetops.

When you reach the large clump of trees where the road bears right, you will see on your left a footpath that goes through the wood. On the other side of the grove this comes out into the **Mile Drive**—a walk that continues straight ahead between two lines of trees. Soon you will reach a dirt road on which you turn right a short distance to the paved road.

Turn left and in a few hundred yards the road will bend to the right. At the next intersection continue straight ahead past the **golf course.** The road then goes down through some trees and swings left along the side of the hill. From here on a clear day a wonderful panorama spreads out before you over the Vale of Evesham and as far as the **Malvern hills.** The village of Broadway stretches out below across the open fields where sheep may be grazing. A few minutes' walk along the road will bring you to the main road that runs into Broadway.

Turn right and follow the sidewalk down the hill until you come to the village. Typical **Cotswold houses** built of yellowish-tan stone line High Street which winds ever so slightly to the far end of Broadway. The name Broadway was presumably derived from an ancient track that ran through the village. As you stroll along, you may think that Broadway consists of nothing but antique stores, art galleries, and gift shops. H. W. Keil is one of the most reliable antique dealers. Some of the low cottages with dormer windows and sloping roofs are Elizabethan. Many have colorful window boxes and tiny gardens facing the street.

The **Lygon Arms,** Broadway's famous inn, is farther down on the right. Built in 1530 it provided hospitality for both Charles I and Oliver Cromwell during the Civil War. Just across from the inn you will see a garage where you can hire a taxi for the return trip to Chipping Campden.

If you feel like wandering a bit more around Broadway and have the time, it will take you a quarter of an hour or so from the Lygon Arms to **St. Eadburgha's Church.** Go down the road to **Snowshill** and you will come to the church on your left. It is cruciform in shape. Much of the church is of Norman origin but the well-proportioned tower and transepts were built towards the end of the thirteenth century. Wander around the imposing interior. The pulpit is a fine example of fourteenth-century woodcarving; there is an Elizabethan palimpsest brass; the font is probably pre-Norman, and many other interesting relics are to be seen.

STOW

In any tour of the Cotswolds the walk from Stow-on-the-World to Bourton-on-the-Water is one you shouldn't miss. Keep off the direct route, the old Roman road, Foss Way, because there is too much traffic, especially in summer.

The route that you should take and will enjoy leads to some of the most charming and characteristic little Cotswold villages —Lower Swell and Upper and Lower Slaughter. The rolling countryside through which you will walk is unusually lovely.

You start in Stow, the highest village of the Cotswolds and finish in one of the most popular, Bourton. But the most scenic and least visited stretch is from Lower Swell to the Slaughters. For these tiny villages with their stone manor houses, cottages, and parish churches have all the attractive qualities that make the Cotswold villages so fascinating.

This walk makes a full morning or afternoon trip—it will probably take you about three hours from the time you leave Stow until you reach Bourton. If you make a late morning start from Stow, you'll be able to have a late lunch in Bourton or even a snack on the way at one of the Slaughters. Try to avoid taking this walk on a Sunday in mid-summer for then Bourton becomes very crowded. If you want to stay in the neighborhood, the **Manor House Hotel** in **Moreton-in-Marsh**—four miles from Stow—is much the best inn. In fact, it is one of the best country hotels in England. Not only does it provide comfortable rooms (many with private bath) and excellent food, but the service is unusually attentive.

Stow-on-the-Wold, 760 feet above sea level on a prominent hilltop, is at the hub of a wheel from which roads radiate to different places in the Cotswolds. It is aptly named because one

117

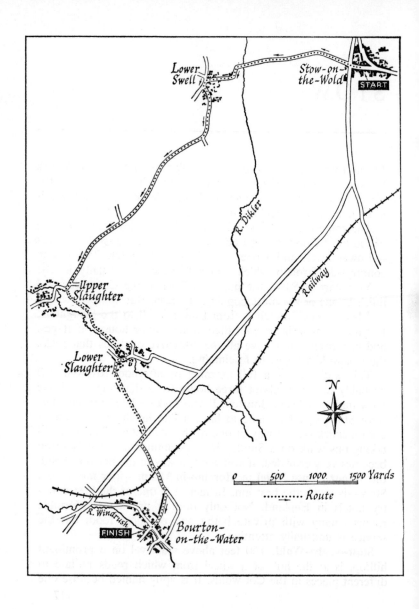

meaning of Stow is meeting place. A market town since 1096, Stow has been famous for centuries for its great fairs, especially during the days when the Cotswold wool industry flourished. Then 20,000 sheep are said to have changed hands at a single Stow fair.

You can park your car in the large **Market Square.** A huge elm towers over one side of the square near the **Red Lion Inn.** Just across the square is an antique shop. In the center stands the Victorian **St. Edward's Hall,** the town's museum and library, where you will see a tablet commemorating the last important battle of the Civil War fought near Stow in 1645. The exhibits include paintings and armor of this period. The old **market cross** is at the far end of the square.

The **parish church** of St. Edward, near St. Edward's Hall, dates from the tenth century. Its pinnacled tower, a landmark for miles around, was built in the middle of the fifteenth century.

After wandering around the square with its gift shops and tearooms, take the narrow street beyond the church at the end of the square and then turn right past the **Unicorn,** Stow's leading inn.

Just across the main road you will see a road marked Cheltenham. There is a twenty minute walk on this road—usually not heavily traveled—first beside grassy banks and stone walls and then bordered by tall trees. The road descends from Stow on the hilltop to the valley of the **River Dikler,** a small stream which you cross just before reaching Lower Swell. If you turn right in the village, you will come to the **parish church,** which is partly Norman and built on the site of a Roman crematorium.

From the triangular green, in the center of the village, follow the road marked Upper Slaughter up a slight rise. Stow's church tower stands out prominently in the distance. At the fork you keep right on the narrow paved road. A great expanse of undulating country opens up on your left. Fields and woods dip down to the valley of the Dikler and rise to the far ridges. Here and there you will spot great manor houses and adjacent farm buildings. Along the top a strong breeze blows across the hills. You will feel invigorated both by the air and the lovely views both near and far over the beautiful Cotswold country-side. In a nearby field a spreading hawthorn stands in solitary splendor above a hedgerow. Continue along the crest and soon the road will begin to descend to Upper Slaughter. As you walk along this stretch there is a striking view of the valley in which the village lies on the banks of a little stream.

Upper Slaughter has been settled since the days of the early Britons before the Roman occupation. The name Slaughter is believed to come from two Saxon words meaning sole-tree, many of which still grow in the vicinity.

After crossing the stream, keep to your left and you will pass a high wall. Behind this stands the **Manor House,** one of the finest in the Cotswolds, part Elizabethan and part fifteenth century. Bear right in the center of the village by the square and follow a little passage a bit further on to the **parish church.** Originally built about 1160, the church is Norman and Early English in style. The fourteenth-century tower has one famous bell, called the **"Eleanor Bell,"** cast during the reign of King Edward I and his queen Eleanor. Three of the chancel windows are of the fourteenth century. The churchyard, planted with clipped yews, overlooks the cottages and farm buildings along the winding streamside. In summer the gardens are ablaze with roses.

Return to the tiny square and retrace your steps along the road beside the manor house to the end of the high stone wall. Turn right on a footpath and go through a swinging wooden gate. Keep slightly to the right as you climb the hill in the pasture towards the tall trees on top. Continue on to the next gate which leads to another meadow. The little stream is down the hill a couple of hundred yards to your right. The path now leads through swinging gates and more fields. Presently you will be on a path that runs along the bank of the stream. In the distance straight ahead beyond those few luxurious tall trees that break the monotony of open fields, you will see the slender spire of the church in **Lower Slaughter.** One more swing gate and you will be in the village. On your right is **the old mill,** no longer in operation but still picturesque with its brick walls rising above the stream. The wheel and machinery are still in working order and now used chiefly for hoisting storage.

Why not stop in at the village store and post office for a snack? Just below the mill the little stream flows right through the center of the village. Though narrow roads run along both sides of the stream—just a few yards back from the grassy banks—you feel as if the stream itself were the village's main street. Stand here on the bank or on one of the low **stone footbridges.** In one direction you look upstream to the old mill and in the other you see the clear stream winding through the village towards the church. Low stone cottages with their colorful gardens sit back just the right distance from the grassy banks. The whole effect of the little village built around the stream is one of the most beautiful you will see anywhere in England. This is an ideal spot to sit for a while on the bank and rest. Usually there is hardly a person about—the only sound is the flow of the water. Here and there narrow **wooden footbridges** cross the stream. Downstream tall trees with their luxurious foliage almost hide the church steeple.

Just below the village green you will come to the church on your left, which was rebuilt in 1866. Take the paved footpath that follows the stream and goes off to the right of the road. After passing through a swinging gate you continue on the path across a big pasture to another swinging gate. At the far side of the next field you reach the main road.

Here you turn right for about a hundred yards, then follow the road to the left, which goes over the railway line that is no longer in use. Now go down the steps to the paved footpath lined with trees. You will pass playing fields on your left and a school on your right. Just beyond the church turn left into the village of **Bourton-on-the-Water.**

Bourton's appeal lies in its parklike setting. The **River Windrush** flows through the center of this large village but, unlike Lower Slaughter, well-kept greens on either side of the river are sufficiently wide so that a little park divides one side of the village from the other. Quaint **stone bridges** (one dating from 1756) span the stream.

Wander about the park and into some of the lanes on either side. Here you will find interesting old cottages and quaint shops.

Several exhibits and attractions have drawn large numbers of tourists. Though these crowds—especially on a Sunday in summer—make the village too trippery, you may be fortunate to come on a weekday when you can see Bourton to better advantage. Some of the exhibits are well worth visiting.

Next to the old **New Inn** is the **Model Village,** a replica of Bourton, one-ninth in size. You will find it fascinating to stroll about the buildings (all made of Cotswold stone) and the grounds which are such accurate reproductions of the original. The miniature trees and gardens are particularly remarkable.

You should also visit **Birdland Zoo Gardens,** a well-designed natural garden of two and a half acres devoted to exhibiting 600 species of foreign birds in their natural habitat. The grounds are imaginatively laid out and many of the exhibits, especially the **Tropical House,** are interesting not only for their glorious birds but luxurious and colorful plants, shrubs, and flowers.

Both the Model Village and Birdland are particularly popular with children.

There are several hotels and inns in Bourton where you can have lunch. Buses leave Bourton for Stow on weekdays at 2:52 (Wednesdays, 2:30) and 5:37. Sundays the buses leave at 1:50, 3:47, and 6:37. The return trip only takes ten minutes or so. You should check the schedule for any changes in time of departure. Or you can probably get a taxi by inquiring at the old New Inn.

STRATFORD

Stratford-on-Avon, the birthplace of William Shakespeare, and scene of the annual Shakespeare Theatre Festival, probably attracts more foreign tourists than any other English town outside of London. Approximately a million visitors come to Stratford every year. More than half are from overseas. Of this number one out of every two is American. So you are pretty certain to visit this pleasant and historic market town in the pastoral valley of the Avon. Ninety miles and less than two hours by train from London, Stratford is a convenient center for visits to **Warwick Castle** and **Coventry Cathedral.** Though Stratford owes its world prominence to Shakespeare, it has a long history going back to the days of Roman Britain. But the charm of Stratford is that it has remained a small country town unspoiled by industrial development. Its location on the river, its many Tudor black-and-white houses and the excellence of the Shakespearean restorations add greatly to the feeling that the spirit of Elizabethan and Shakespearean England still lives in Stratford.

Largely as a result of the efforts of the Shakespeare Birthplace Trust, those buildings most associated with the poet's days in Stratford have been extremely well restored and preserved as a national memorial.

In planning your visit to Stratford, you should make advance reservations to attend the outstanding repertory performances of the Royal Shakespeare Company which take place from early spring to late autumn.

There are two walks in Stratford which you will enjoy. The first will take you to the major places in the town which are associated with Shakespeare. The second is to the neighboring village of Shottery to visit **Anne Hathaway's** charming cottage.

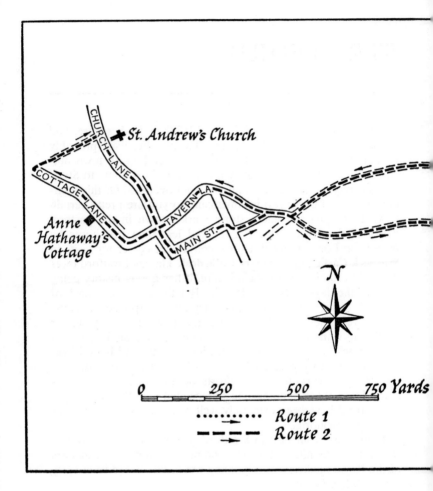

St. Andrew's Church

CHURCH LANE

COTTAGE LANE

Anne
Hathaway's
Cottage

TAVERN LA.

MAIN ST.

N

0   250   500   750 Yards

•••••••→ Route 1
– – –→ Route 2

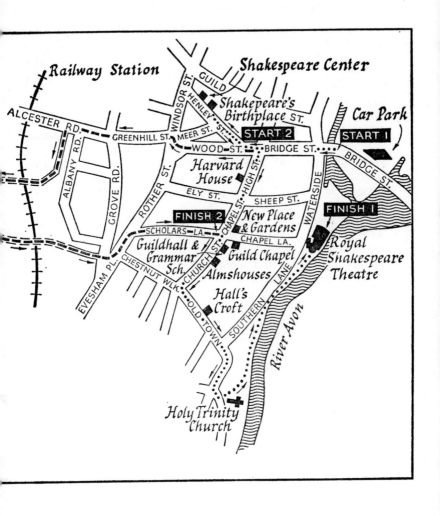

Commence your stroll through Stratford along the Avon whose banks are bordered with green parks and colorful gardens. Start from the late medieval **Clopton Bridge,** built at the end of the fifteenth century by Hugh Clopton, a native of Stratford who became Lord Mayor of London. From this ancient stone bridge with fourteen arches you have a good view on your left of the well-proportioned **Memorial Theatre,** which on one side overlooks the river and in front the pleasant **Bancroft Gardens.**

Continue ahead on **Bridgefoot** (there's a large car park on your right) past the **Shakespeare monument.** The four statues surrounding the figure of the poet depict philosophy, history, comedy, and tragedy in the form of Hamlet, Prince Hal, Falstaff, and Lady Macbeth.

Go straight ahead up **Bridge Street** past the **Red Horse Hotel** on your right. At the intersection beyond bear right on **Henley Street** and in a short distance you will come to the sixteenth-century **half-timbered building** where Shakespeare was born in 1564 (open weekdays, 9:00–6:00; Sundays, 10:00–6:00 April–October; weekdays, 9:00–12:45; 2:00–4:00; Sundays, 2:00–4:00 November–March. On Thursdays and Saturdays and each weekday in June through September the closing time is 7 P.M.). Despite its restoration, the house looks substantially the same as it did four hundred years ago. Also, it retains quite a lot of the original timber framing. It was built of local materials—timber from the nearby Forest of Arden and blue-gray stone from Wilmcote where Shakespeare's mother lived. As was customary during the Tudor period, wattle and daub was used to fill the spaces between the timbers.

When the Shakespeare family lived here, there were two separate buildings. The western one was the family home and the house next door was the shop where Shakespeare's father used to carry on his trade as a wool dealer and glover. The entire house has now been furnished in Elizabethan and Jacobean style to recreate to some degree the atmosphere in which the Shakespeare family lived. Note the interesting early brick and stone **fireplace** in the living room. Not greatly changed since Shakespeare's day. The **kitchen** with its great open hearth and cooking utensils of the period looks much as it must have been during Shakespeare's time.

The **museum** upstairs contains exhibits of early editions of Shakespeare's plays, portraits of the poet, manuscripts, books, and documents relating to Shakespeare's life and works. Don't miss the old-fashioned **school desk** from the Stratford grammar school which Shakespeare is said to have used.

In the room where it is believed Shakespeare was born, nearly all of the timber work is original as is the fireplace. You can see the ancient wattle and daub construction in one of the panels. The original glass windowpanes reveal the names of prominent visitors, such as Sir Walter Scott, Thomas Carlyle, Henry Irving, and Ellen Terry. Just outside the birthroom are the original family stairs.

Wander about in the delightful **garden.** Here trees, herbs, plants, and flowers which Shakespeare mentioned in his plays and poems have been artistically planted as well as a wide herbaceous border.

Next to the birthplace is a modern building of interesting design called the **Shakespeare Center,** opened in 1964 to commemorate the 400th anniversary of Shakespeare's birth. It was erected to house a Shakespearean library and lecture rooms and is well worth visiting. The incised etchings on glass panels are particularly fine and were created by the same artist John Hutton who did similar work at Coventry Cathedral.

Retrace your steps up **Henley Street** and turn right at the roundabout on High Street. On your left you will pass overhanging Elizabethan stucco and timber houses. A few yards further on the right you will come to **Harvard House** (open weekdays, 9:00–1:00; 2:00–6:00; Sundays, 2:00–6:00), a Tudor timber and stucco building with the best exterior wood carving in Stratford. Built in 1596 by a grandfather of John Harvard, it now belongs to the University which he founded. There is fine linenfold oak paneling in the front room on the first floor, now occupied by the local chapter of the English-Speaking Union. Go up to the top floor to see the original oak beams and a most unusual view over the old tiled roofs of

Stratford. Two black and white Tudor buildings adjoin Harvard House.

Cross over High Street at the corner of **Ely Street.** Just past the half-timbered **Shakespeare Hotel** (1555) on **Chapel Street** is the Stratford Information Office. Beyond it you will come to **New Place** where Shakespeare lived during his last years and died in 1616.

Originally one of Stratford's most imposing homes when Shakespeare bought it in 1597, today only the brick foundations remain in the front garden. Low plants and flowers brighten the otherwise dreary remains of the house. You enter the grounds through **Nash's House,** a sixteenth-century half-timbered building once owned by Shakespeare's granddaughter. Here is an interesting collection of furniture and other objects of Shakespearean England as well as a local **museum** with exhibits of the Roman and Anglo-Saxon periods (same hours as Shakespeare's Birthplace, except it never stays open after 6 P.M.)

After looking at the foundations of Shakespeare's house, stroll into the charming **Elizabethan Knott garden,** typical of fine homes during Shakespeare's lifetime. Surrounded by a luxurious square hedge and slightly sunken, the garden consists of four "knotts" or beds, planted with flowers and herbs in an intricate pattern. After wandering about this lovely spot, go on to the **great garden** behind with its spacious lawns, magnificent beech, and borders of box and yew hedges. There is also a mulberry tree descended from a cutting which Shakespeare planted here. From the grounds you have a fine view of the house, the Guild Chapel and the black-and-white **Falcon Hotel** across Chapel Street. This is a delightful spot to relax for a while from sightseeing.

The **Guild Chapel,** largely remodeled during the fifteenth century, is one of Stratford's most historic buildings and one that undoubtedly was well known to Shakespeare. Go inside to see a fine **fresco** over the chancel arch. This "Doom" or Last Judgement is one of the largest surviving versions in Britain. Originally all the walls were covered with similar frescoes and it seems that John Shakespeare, the poet's father, was obliged to supervise the defacement of these decorations when he served as Chamberlain to the Corporation of Stratford in 1563

Next door to the chapel stands a half-timbered building built 1416–1418. The lower floor was Stratford's original **Guildhall** and the upper floor has housed the **Grammar School** which Shakespeare probably attended. Shakespeare's interest in drama may have been aroused here by performances given in the Guildhall by companies of traveling players. Next door are the fifteenth-century **almshouses** where twenty-four aged local inhabitants live in this long row of half-timbered buildings with an overhanging upper story.

At the end of the block, turn left on **Old Town. Hall's Croft** is midway down the block on your left.

Hall's Croft, a large distinguished timber-framed building, one of the finest old houses in Stratford, was the home of Shakespeare's elder daughter, Susanna, and her husband, Dr. John Hall (open same hours as Birthplace except that it never stays open after 6 P.M.). Aside from the Birthplace, this is the most interesting sixteenth-century house in Stratford. The exterior, with its overhanging upper story, gabled roofs, and picturesque chimneys, is most attractive. Inside you will be fascinated not only by the outstanding collection of late Tudor and early Jacobean **furniture** but also a **dispensary** of the period with equipment, herbals, medicines, etc., as used in Shakespeare's day. Be sure to wander around the beautifully planted **garden** with its fine flower borders and extensive lawn. During the theatrical season the Festival Club, offering restaurant and lounge facilities to visitors, occupies part of the building.

Walk along Old Town to the end of the street, then bear right along an avenue of tall lime trees to **Holy Trinity Church.** Cruciform in design, the church dates from about 1210. The **knocker** on the porch door is an old sanctuary ring which entitled a criminal reaching it to claim protection for 37 days. To the right of the door as you enter, you will see in a case the pages of the **parish register** that show the entries of Shakespeare's baptism and burial. The nearby fifteenth-century **font** is the one in which it is believed the poet was baptized. **Shakespeare's grave,** marked by a stone slab with the famous inscription, and above it the earliest known statue of the poet done about 1623, are in the chancel on your left as you face the High Altar. Before leaving the church, look at the old **chained Bible** (1611) in the southwest corner.

Stroll for a while about the churchyard—it is particularly attractive behind the church where you may see the church spire mirrored in the waters of the Avon. A few steps from the entrance to the churchyard will bring you into the **waterside gardens** (open 9:00–5:00) of the Shakespeare Memorial Theatre. The theatre grounds, with its colorful flower border and wide lawn running down to the river, are very pleasant indeed. You will probably see numerous swans swimming by the punts and canoes.

You might conclude this walk through Stratford by visiting the Memorial Theatre **Picture Gallery and Museum** (open weekdays, 10:00–1:00; Sundays, 2:00–6:00 April to November) to see the collection of portraits connected with Shakespeare and his plays. The exhibit also includes **Shakespeare's gloves,** which David Garrick presented in 1769, and theatrical relics of Garrick, Sir Henry Irving, and other distinguished Shakespearean actors.

The second walk to **Anne Hathaway's cottage** will take about a half hour from the roundabout in Bridge Street. You start along **Wood Street.** When you reach a large square, cross it and go straight ahead past a black-and-white house on **Greenhill Street.** Continue along Greenhill Street and just beyond Albany Road before the railway overpass, turn sharply to your left down a footpath marked "To Anne Hathaway's Cottage." Shortly the footpath will cross the railway tracks. Follow the paved path across a meadow and sports ground. When you reach a road, follow the sign straight ahead and in about a hundred yards bear right to the cottage.

Anne Hathaway's Cottage (open same hours as Shakespeare's Birthplace) is a long, low, remarkably well-preserved timber-framed sixteenth-century farmhouse with thatched roof. The **garden** around the cottage is one of the most beautiful you will see and provides a perfect setting for this home where the Hathaway family lived from Shakespeare's day until 1892 when it was acquired by the Shakespeare Birthplace Trust. There are original oak beams and stone flooring inside the house, which is furnished with period pieces. Among the ancient kitchen utensils on display is a sixteenth-century trencher—a round wooden board used as a plate—from which the term trencherman is derived. In the hall is a "courting" settle or high-backed bench on which Shakespeare and Anne Hathaway are supposed to have sat.

When you leave the Hathaway Cottage, go left and you'll pass some delightful old houses. Cross the road and go down the paved footpath past several thatched cottages until in about two hundred yards you come to **St. Andrew's Church, Shottery.** Turn right on **Church Lane** and shortly you will pass two charming cottages with black oak beams, brickwork painted white, and thatched roofs. Each sits back from the road and is surrounded by an inviting garden.

At the crossroads you can catch a bus to return to Stratford. If you walk back (you can return on a different footpath in about half an hour), keep right past some thatched black and white cottages, then go left on a paved footpath along a red brick wall. After going through a gate, bear right on the footpath and on the far side of the pasture go through the next stile gate and across the railway tracks. Turn left at **Evesham Place** on the far side of a triangular park, then a few yards on **Rother Street** take the first street to the right—**Scholars Lane**—which will bring you into Chapel Street opposite New Place.

CHESTER

Chester is planned for people who like to walk. Nowhere else in England do you have to walk to enjoy the city's special tourist attractions. Chester's unique features are its city wall and its Rows. Both are made to order for the visitor who likes to walk.

The **city walls**—forty feet high in places—completely encircle this historic community. You can have an intensely interesting two-mile walk along the ancient ramparts from which you will have fine views of Chester and the surrounding country. Parts of the walls are built on **Roman foundations.** Other parts cross Chester's main streets at the various ancient **city gates.** At frequent intervals **medieval towers** still stand as a reminder of the days when Chester was a fortified town.

The Rows, however, are more unusual and are unique in England. They are arcades or continuous promenades built at the second-story level on Chester's four main streets. Shops line the inner side of the arcade and balustrades overlook the street which you can reach by frequent stairways. Chester's Rows go back at least to 1331. Although the reason for their medieval origin is uncertain, it is generally accepted that the Rows were built above the street level because the massive ruins of Roman buildings impeded easy passage. Their relationship with Roman Chester seems clear, for the Rows only exist in the area of the Roman city. The practicality of the Rows for the English climate was described by the Rev. John Wesley who wrote that by means of "these covered galleries one may walk both clean and dry in any weather, from one end of the city to another."

Two thousand years ago (60 A.D.) the twentieth Roman legion built a fortress as its headquarters on the site of Chester. The town—Deva—remained one of the most important and

132

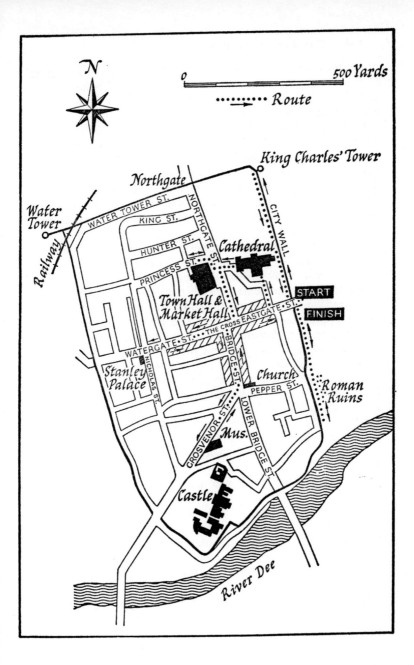

prosperous communities in Roman Britain until the departure of the Romans at the end of the fourth century. Chester's name is derived from the Roman "castra" or camp and Roman relics are continually being uncovered in the modern city.

Chester, as you see it today, retains a number of black and white half-timbered Tudor and Stuart houses particularly along Lower Bridge Street and Watergate Street. The fronts of the buildings on Chester's four main streets, built on Roman foundations, are now an interesting mixture of architectural styles. The few timber-framed buildings with Georgian facades and soaring black and white beams might best be described as Victorian Elizabethan.

Start your walking tour of Chester at the **Eastgate,** the city's main entrance. The present archway was constructed on Roman foundations in 1769. Go up the stairs just beside the archway. Pause for a few moments beneath the great Victorian clock to look over the stream of traffic that crowds busy Eastgate, Chester's shopping center. From here you get an excellent view of the mixture of architectural styles in Chester. Then turn right along the city wall. In a moment you will have an unusually fine view of the cathedral on your left. A few hundred yards further will bring you to **King Charles's Tower** (open, May through September, 10:00–6:30 Monday–Friday; 10:00–7:00 Saturday; 2:30–6:30 Sunday). Here King Charles I watched the defeat of his troops by Parliamentary soldiers at the Battle of Rowton Heath in 1645. Inside you will see dioramas illustrating the battle and siege of Chester. Also on exhibit are armor, artillery, and other Civil War relics.

If you are in the mood, you may want to continue along the wall for a while. In a few minutes you will cross **Northgate.** At the northwest corner of the walls you will reach the **Water Tower** (opening times similar to those for King Charles's Tower) overlooking the river whose waters at one time surrounded it. Dioramas of medieval Chester on exhibit in the tower are most interesting. Stroll back along the walls to Eastgate.

Before descending the stairs into Eastgate, proceed along the walls past the clock until, in a few hundred yards, you reach a point where you see below you on your left remains of Roman Chester. Just beside the **Wolfe Gate** you will see a lawn with excavated portions of the Roman wall. **Roman columns** have been re-erected nearby. You also will notice Chester's **High Cross** reconstructed from fragments of the original cross that once stood in the center of the city before its destruction during the Civil War.

Returning to Eastgate you go down the stairway and walk along the main street inside the wall. This street was the Roman Watling Street that ran to London. As you stroll along, look above you at the richly carved beams, bay windows, overhanging balconies and black and white effect of the **Tudor buildings.** Just before you reach the Rows on the right-hand side, turn right into **St. Werburgh Street.** The building on the right with its peaked gables is a particularly interesting example of Victorian Elizabethan architecture. Keep to the left along this street, named for St. Werburgh, patron saint of Chester Cathedral and famed for her devotion to Christianity. You will pass **Chester Cathedral** on your right. Before you enter it, have a look at the interesting **covered walk** on the left with its shops. The building with a **Gothic facade** which you see ahead is now a supermarket. Originally it was built in the fourteenth century as a chapel and later it was the Common Hall of the City before being used as a theatre.

Although a church stood on the site of Chester Cathedral almost a thousand years ago, the present building is of Norman origin. In 1093 Hugh Lupus, nephew of William the Conqueror, began the Benedictine Abbey, which displaced an earlier Saxon Church. Parts of the Norman Abbey remain on the cathedral's north side.

Enter the great, red sandstone cathedral through the **south porch** from St. Werburgh Street. You will come into the south transept with four chapels. In the corner chapel to your right hangs the Cheshire regiment's flag in which General Wolfe's body was wrapped at the Battle of Quebec and which was later carried at the Battle of Bunker Hill.

After looking at the **nave** and the twelfth-century **Baptistry,** go into the **choir,** the glory of the cathedral, to see the magnificent **canopied stalls.** The carving of the late fourteenth-century woodwork with its tall spires and pinnacles is indeed exquisite. Don't leave the choir without studying the marvelous woodcarving of the Dean's and Vice-Dean's stalls as well as the bench-ends. The exceptional and amusing carving on the **misericords** —forty-two of the forty-eight are original—reflects the spirit of the Middle Ages. The **Shrine of St. Werburgh,** where pilgrims prayed for healing miracles, is at the west end of the Lady Chapel behind the high altar.

Stroll about the **cloister** with its attractive garth and pool, then visit the fine thirteenth-century **Chapter House** on the right. Here you will find treasures of the cathedral library, including a copy of the *Polychronicon,* a chronicle of history written by Ralph Higden in the fourteenth century. There are also other manuscripts, a twelfth-century Bible, and a fifteenth-century Book of Hours on view by special request. The **refectory,** off the cloisters, is the best preserved part of the fourteenth-century abbey and has an exquisite early English pulpit from which the monks read during meals to the brethren. The new stalls in the nave, and the great **West Window** inserted in 1961 are worth inspection.

You leave the cathedral buildings through **Abbey Square** with its circular green and terraced eighteenth-century houses. In this square the **Chester miracle plays** were enacted. Go through the great abbey gateway to Northgate.

Cross the busy street and next to the **Town Hall** you will enjoy wandering through the new public market. Here everything from meat, fish, and vegetables to clothing and household utensils is on sale. It's a lively, gay place and provides a pleasant change of pace from the austere, ecclesiastical atmosphere of the cathedral.

After touring the market, turn right on **North Street** along the Row. This street-level Row was built in 1897. Stop in at the Nola dress shop at No. 23 and ask permission to go down into the basement to see some interesting Roman remains. The excavated bases, shafts, and columns were part of the Roman military headquarters building.

Back on Northgate, you continue to your right and in a few yards will come to **St. Peter's Church** on the corner. While you are strolling along, look opposite to the balconied black and white houses. The city's High Cross used to stand in front of St. Peter's at the juncture of Chester's four main streets. This is the center of the city and still called **The Cross.** The church itself occupies part of the site of the Roman military headquarters.

From this point you can get an excellent idea of the Rows. Diagonally across the street on the corner, a stairway leads to the arcades which run above the street-level shops and beneath the colorful buildings with their overhanging stories, gabled windows, and peaked roofs.

Cross Watergate to No. 11, for here you can visit a fascinating **double crypt,** built about 1180 and now used by Quellyn Roberts & Co. Ltd., wine merchants. Wander back in the crypt where casks of Scotch whiskey line the walls beneath the ancient arches.

The **Watergate Rows** are among the finest in Chester, for this street led to the port, an active trading center until it was displaced by Liverpool. Next door to the ancient crypt is the sixteenth-century **Leche House,** one of the least altered in Chester, and now an antiques shop. Dr. Samuel Johnson stayed here at one time. You can walk through the shop to the charming little garden in back. (It is so typical of England to find such a delightful spot hidden away.) Here sixteenth-century oak beams support a black and white upper story that was a lady's bower in Tudor times. Go upstairs to see **the squint,** which permitted people to look into the banqueting hall below. There is also a **minstrel's gallery** and a hiding place for priests at the top of the fireplace.

A few steps along the Rows will bring you to **Bishop Lloyd's house.** Its carved oak facade is the most elaborate in Chester. Stand across Watergate and look up at the panels. Many are of animals; some are biblical in character; on one is carved J.R.

for James I; all are superbly fashioned. The founder of Yale University was descended from Bishop Lloyd's eldest daughter.

Continue along Watergate to **Nicholas Street** and across it on the corner you will come to **Stanley Palace,** a distinguished late sixteenth-century house, now the Chester Branch of the English-Speaking Union. After looking around its paneled rooms, return along Watergate to The Cross.

Turn right on Bridge Street and stroll along this Row past the twisted pillars of the seventeenth-century **"Dutch" houses.** Bear right on Lower Grosvenor Street for a few hundred yards to visit the **Grosvenor Museum** (open weekdays, 10:00–5:00; 2:30–5:00 Sundays in summer). In addition to its archeological and natural history collection, you will see interesting exhibits of Roman Chester with models and various excavated relics. This section on the Roman occupation is most instructive.

Return along **Grosvenor Street** and then turn right at the corner in **Lower Bridge Street** by the **Falcon,** an early seventeenth-century black and white building. Cross over to **St. Michael's Church** built on the site of a Roman fort and resume your stroll along St. Michael's arcade, one of the Rows. You will find small interesting shops, especially those specializing in antiques and curios. You might want to go into **Lawleys,** a china shop at No. 39, to see the Roman baths and hypocaust, a low cellarlike cavity used to keep houses warm and dry. Continue along the Row to the corner opposite The Cross and then turn right and finish your tour of Chester by strolling along **Eastgate Row,** which has some of the finest shops in the city. From here it is only a few hundred yards to the clock tower at Eastgate.

YORK I

York during the Middle Ages was the second largest city in England—a position it held until the seventeenth century. Today as you stand in admiration before the world-renowned Minster, wander through York's narrow, irregular streets, or stroll along its ancient walls, you still feel the medieval influence. Despite the ever present reminders of the modern day, old York has succeeded in preserving its ancient character. Its Roman foundations, Norman fortress, medieval city walls and massive gateways, old churches, quaint houses, parks with ancient abbey ruins, and historic guildhalls will give you some sense of York's place in the stream of English history. York is full of interest, so don't make the mistake of thinking that the Minster and the Shambles—York's famous medieval street—are all that is worth seeing here.

York is a perfect city to wander in—you are almost bound to find yourself in an enchanting little street or an out-of-the-way corner with a delightful view of the Minster wherever you turn. If you saunter along the Lendal Bridge by the River Ouse, the effect of the buildings rising above the stream will make you think of cities on the Continent. A stroll along the walls will reveal delightful glimpses of old houses and charming gardens with the towers of the Minster as a dramatic backdrop. The most interesting old section of the city is in one rather small area so the places you want to see are close at hand.

York in northeast England is on the usual motor route up the east coast to Scotland. You can drive the approximately two hundred miles from London in a comfortable day's trip on double carriageways or expressways. By rail York is on the

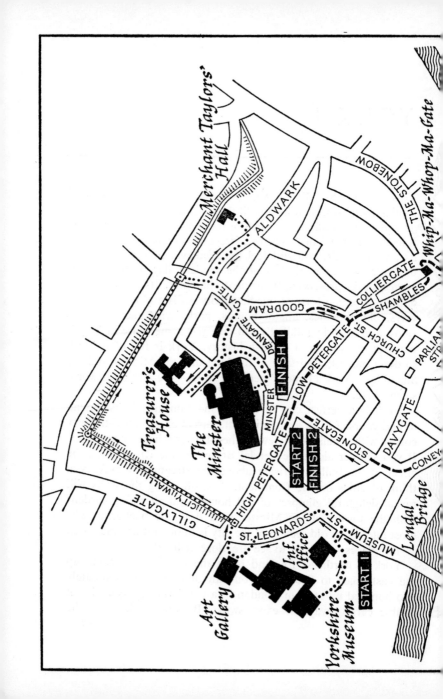

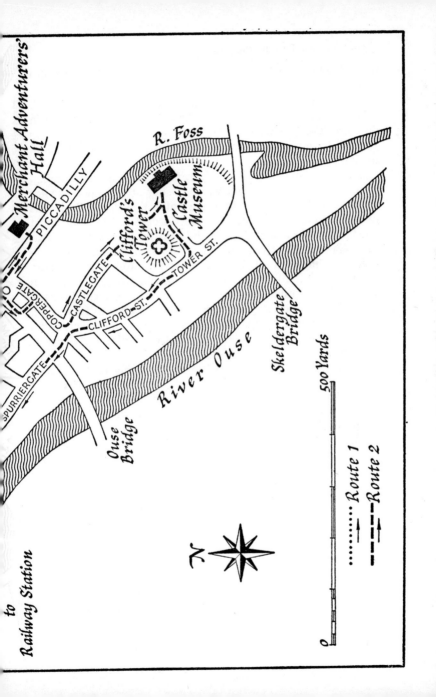

main line between London (less than three hours by fast train) and Edinburgh.

There is so much to see in **York** that two walks are suggested, each of which should take about half a day. Neither is long in distance. The first walk—quite short—ends at the Minster, so you will have plenty of time to enjoy this magnificent cathedral, the largest in England.

Start your first walk, if possible, fairly early in the morning, for on a clear day the light will be better at that hour to view the towers of the Minster from the walls. You should begin this tour at the entrance to the **Museum Gardens** on Museum Street not far from **Lendal Bridge.** Stroll into the pleasant park that runs down to the river. Here you will find the restored **Hospitium,** a museum of Roman antiquities (open in summer, 10:30–12:30; 2:00–5:00). Roman York dates from 71 A.D. when a fortress was established on the site of the present Minster. Known during the 340 years of Roman occupation as Eboracum, York was visited by the Emperors Hadrian and Severus and was the scene of the proclamation of Constantine the Great as Emperor.

From the Hospitium, walk up to the ruins of **St. Mary's Abbey,** founded in 1089 and Yorkshire's first monastery after the Norman Conquest. Now visit the adjacent **Yorkshire Museum** (open weekdays, 10:00–5:00). In addition to its fine exhibits of Roman remains, there are archeological, geological, and natural history collections as well as galleries of Saxon, Danish, and medieval antiquities. Don't miss the eighth-century silver-gilt Anglian **Ormside bowl.**

The most historic and best preserved bit of Roman York is the **Multangular Tower** on your left as you return to the park entrance from the museum. This is one of the corner bastions of the Roman fortress and part of the early fourth-century **Roman wall** which is about four or five feet thick. The lower Roman section can be identified from the upper medieval wall by its smaller facing stones. At the end of the wall stands the thirteenth-century remains of **St. Leonard's Hospital.**

Turning left on Museum Street, you will pass the **Public**

Library in a few yards. Here the local tourist information office is located on the ground floor. Voluntary guides are usually available each afternoon to conduct groups of visitors on walking tours of the city during the summer. To the left of the library entrance you can get a closer look at the Multangular Tower and Roman wall.

Now bear left on **St. Leonard's Place** past eighteenth-century houses. Almost opposite the **Theatre Royal** you will notice more remains of the Roman wall, a portion of the legionary fortress built in the fourth century. **King's Manor** on the left, behind a large courtyard and lawn, was originally (1280) the residence of the abbot of St. Mary's, then was converted to a Tudor palace, and now is part of the University of York. Just a bit further on the left is the **City Art Gallery** (open weekdays, 10:00–5:00; Sundays, 2:30–5:00; during the summer months it closes daily at 8:00), a collection with particular stress on the Italian and Dutch schools. Some of the modern paintings upstairs are interesting.

After this introduction to York—mostly the York of Roman days—you now approach the city's **ramparts.** Opposite the art gallery stands the solid bulk of battlemented **Bootham Bar,** the gate that led to the north from which direction came York's ancient and most dangerous enemies.

Before you climb up the steps at Bootham Bar leading to the **walk around the wall,** notice the **portcullis** under the gateway. This stretch of the fourteenth-century wall is particularly delightful and the most enjoyable of all sections of the city's walls. The walk is wide and made attractive by trees and flowering shrubs. While you stroll along, you have lovely views of the Minster's towers above the old roofs. From this vantage point, a tranquil air seems to settle over the city. You are removed from all the noise of traffic and left alone to contemplate the beauty of the charming gardens, old houses, and the majestic Minster. On your right, the large brick house and lovely garden belong to **the Deanery.** On your left, after you turn the corner, you will see the remains of the **moat.**

Descend at **Monk Bar,** which was erected on Roman foundations about 1230–1250. A few steps from Monk Bar on **Good-ramgate** turn left on **Aldwark** to visit the **Merchant Taylors' Hall** (open weekdays, 10:00–5:00). This late fourteenth-century hall became in 1415 the property of the Craft of Tailors, one of York's earliest city guilds. Its spacious hall, set back behind a broad lawn, has a remarkably fine late fourteenth-century timber roof.

Retrace your steps to Goodramgate, turn left and shortly go right on curved **College Street**. On your right is **St. William's College**. A black and white Tudor building with overhanging story, it was established in 1461 for the cathedral's chantry priests. Notice the fine wood carving of the restored outer doorway. If you look carefully you will find a little figure of a mouse, the trademark of a prominent contemporary wood carver, in the upper corner of the outside door. Go into the cobbled inner quadrangle, which is early Georgian. You can also see interesting seventeenth-century stairs and an open timber roof in the principal chamber.

Continue past St. William's College and keep right into **Minster Yard** behind the cathedral to the **Treasurer's House** (open weekdays, except Wednesday morning, 10:00–1:00; 2:00–6:00, until 4:00 from October–March; Sundays June, July, August, 10:00–1:00; 2:00–6:00; December, January, February closed).

Built originally at the end of the eleventh century on the site of the Roman barracks, the house as it stands today is mainly post-seventeenth century. It is a most beautifully proportioned building and has been tastefully furnished with fine period furniture and works of art. Now owned by the National Trust, it is well worth visiting, especially for those who admire seventeenth- and eighteenth-century furniture and interior decoration. The grounds are also most attractive.

Walk around **the Minster** to view this most spectacular cathedral from its splendid **west front**. The present structure, begun about 1220, is the fifth cathedral to be built on this site. King Edwin of Northumbria put up a wooden chapel and was baptized here in 627. Pause for a few moments to study the superb stonework of the portals and the entire magnificent **facade,** one of the finest in all Europe.

When you enter, the vastness of the Minster's interior will impress you at once. But York's outstanding characteristic is its treasure of medieval **stained glass,** unequaled in England. Turn back to view the great **west window** with its amazingly beautiful flamboyant tracery. When you reach a point beneath the central tower, look to your left in the north transept at York's most famous glass windows, **the Five Sisters.** These are the largest lancet windows in the world. Their grisaille (grayish-green) glass is thirteenth century and is said to consist of 100,-000 separate pieces of glass. York Minster's extraordinary collection of medieval glass is a treasure unrivaled in England and renowned throughout the world.

To the right of the north transept you will find the **Chapter House,** a very beautifully proportioned original chamber and considered one of the finest in the country. Its **pyramidal roof** is unique and its windows have been restored with their original glass. The Saxon Book of the Gospels and Horn of Ulphus are among the treasures on exhibit.

Return to the north transept, then turn left along the north choir aisle. Go in the choir to see the new choir stalls. As you stroll around the choir, you will admire two huge **windows** (St. William and St. Cuthbert) with the world's finest fifteenth-century glass. The largest area of stained glass ever made is the early fifteenth-century **east window** above the Lady Chapel. Seventy-six feet high and thirty-two feet broad, it contains more than two thousand square feet of medieval glass.

Before you leave this glorious cathedral, pause once again beneath the central tower and have a final look at these marvelous stained-glass windows. Their beauty and the vast proportions of the Minster will leave you with a profound sense of humility and awe for the artistry of the Middle Ages.

YORK II

This second walk will take you through **York's** quaint, narrow streets with their old houses and overhanging second stories. In no other large English city have the streets and buildings of medieval days been more successfully preserved on such an extensive scale. Though you will be strolling through the heart of a modern city, at every hand you will find much to remind you of York as it was hundreds of years ago.

Start at the **Church of St. Michael-le-Belfry** just opposite the Minster. Here Guy Fawkes, who attempted to blow up the Houses of Parliament, was baptized. After admiring the church's fine **stained glass,** go out into **High Petergate** and turn left. At the junction of **Stonegate** only a few feet away, note the decorative figure over the corner of the brick building. Just opposite you can see "1646" carved on the corner pillar. An eighteenth-century torch extinguisher is outside the doorway. Continue along **Low Petergate,** built over a Roman road and so named since the thirteenth century, past enticing antique shops. Look back for a dramatic view of the Minster's Towers rising above the peaked and tiled roofs.

Turn left at Goodramgate and go for about fifty yards to a gate on the left leading to the odd little church of **Holy Trinity** in the midst of an ancient **churchyard.** The houses on your right are among the oldest in York. Although the foundations of Holy Trinity date from the thirteenth century, the present building is about a hundred years later. You will be interested in the church's uneven flooring, its seventeenth-century "box" pews and its lovely east window (1472).

Return to the junction of Low Petergate and Goodramgate, then bear left into flag-stoned **Kings Square.** Go past the circular

rookery and by the old corner building whose upper story rests on wooden beams taken from Elizabethan ships, you come to the famous **Shambles.** Just before you stroll into the Shambles, turn right into **King's Court** to an open-air food and clothing market.

Once the street of the butchers, the Shambles takes its name from the stalls on which meat used to be displayed. This fascinating, tiny street—barely wide enough for one car—was mentioned in the Domesday Book, and assumed its present character about 1400. The overhanging upper stories of the timbered houses with their steep gables come so close together that at one point a person could almost lean out the window and shake hands with a neighbor across the street. Nowadays antique and curio shops, jewelers, silversmiths, woodcraftsmen, and other fine stores have made the Shambles rather fashionable. At Number 37 go into an alley to look at this house's ancient timbers. The fifteenth-century hall of the **Butchers' Guild** is upstairs at Nos. 41–42 on your right. This charming hall, with a **vaulted ceiling** whose beams are pegged, was until recently the York branch of the English-Speaking Union.

At the end of the Shambles, go left down a narrow passageway to the **Whip-Ma-Whop-Ma-Gate,** York's shortest street. Here felons were whipped centuries ago.

Turn right along **Pavement** where once a gallows stood and go left at the busy intersection on **Piccadilly** to the historic **Merchant Adventurers' Hall** set back in a lawn below the street level. (Open weekdays, 10:00–12:30; 2:00–5:00 to 6:00, Tuesday, Thursday, Fridays April to October, Tuesday to Saturday 10:00–12:30; 2:00–4:00, except second and third weeks of November from November to March.)

This black and white timbered building, probably the finest medieval guild hall in York, was built in the mid-fourteenth century by the company of mercers who became the Merchant Adventurers a century later. This company, once the most powerful in York, still exists as a charitable organization. The **great hall,** with its elegant high-pitched, half-timbered roof used to be the place where cloth, that the weavers had made on hand-looms at home, was brought for trading and for export. Be sure to visit the ancient **undercroft** with its fourteenth-century windows. It used to be divided into cubicles for the guild's pensioners. The oldest part is the wall along the garden. The company's records for purchase of bricks and stone in 1358 show that 20,000 handmade bricks were bought for seven cents a thousand, which was considered expensive. However, stone at fourteen cents a ton was relatively cheap.

Return to the intersection of Piccadilly and Pavement, then cross over to your left to visit the **Church of All Saints Pavement.** Its prominent and fine fifteenth-century **lantern,** from which a large lamp guided visitors to the city, dominates this part of York. Note the twelfth-century **knocker** on the north door. Inside you will find an ancient carved lectern, fine paneled roof and a fourteenth-century glass west window.

Go left from the church's entrance into adjacent **Coppergate,** then turn right and in a few yards go left at **Castlegate.** In a few moments you will see on your right **Clifford's Tower** on top of a mound which William the Conqueror constructed as a fortress. The remains of the existing stone tower, built in quatrefoil plan, date from the thirteenth century. If you care to climb a long flight of steps, you can walk along its walls (open weekdays and Sundays May to September, 9:30–7:00; weekdays, 9:30–5:30, Sundays March, April, and October 2:00–5:30; to 4:00 weekdays and Sundays November to February).

Just beyond Clifford's Tower you will see the **Castle Museum** (open weekdays, 9:30–7:30, Sundays, 2:00–7:00; from October to March closes at 4:30). Although various sections of this folk museum are of considerable interest, the most remarkable and lifelike part is **Alderman's Walk** and **Kirkgate.** These are reconstructed streets, together with fronts of houses and shops, exactly as they were in Victorian and Edwardian York. In fact, the cobbled street, with its old lampposts and hansom cab, the lighted shops and their windows full of goods which were popular during those days are so realistic that you can hardly believe you have not been transported to York of a century ago. The detail of the buildings and their contents has been so faithfully executed that you will find this living museum to be one of the most fascinating experiences certainly in York and perhaps in your tour of England. The old firehouse, post office, cordwainer, saddles, book shop, and confectionery are all so enticing that you will find one more interesting than the next. The Victorian parlor of 1880 is particularly nostalgic. You can even wander in some of the shops and inspect what your ancestors used to buy.

Before you leave the museum, you may want to see upstairs the attractive **period rooms** of Jacobean, Georgian, and Victorian days.

The adjoining building, an extension of the museum, was formerly the Debtors' Prison. Here you can see on the ground floor a series of **craft workshops** such as a comb and clay-pipe maker, tanner, printer, gunsmith, blacksmith, etc. On the first floor there is a display of eighteenth- and nineteenth-century **costumes.** Don't miss the **toy collection** and doll house which children will find delightful.

The military section on the second floor includes uniforms and arms of the Yorkshire regiments.

Turn left from the museum grounds and after passing Clifford's Tower on the right, you will be in **Clifford Street.** Continue to **Nessgate** and cross over to **Spurriergate,** a busy shopping street. The **Church of St. Michael** on the left-hand corner possesses very fine medieval glass. Walk along Spurriergate and on into **Coney Street.** When you reach **St. Helen's Square** you will see on your left the stately early eighteenth-century **Mansion House** where the Lord Mayor lives. Charming flower baskets hang from the lampposts in front of the creamy stone and maroon-painted brick building. Just behind the Mansion House down a passageway is York's restored **Guildhall** with a fine timbered roof (open Monday–Friday, 9:00–5:30; Saturdays, May to October, 9:00–5:00).

Stroll through St. Helen's Square and just opposite the Mansion House you will enter **Stonegate,** an ancient street that goes back to the twelfth century and now is a center of antique book and fine arts shops. When you stand at the entrance of Stonegate and look along this charming old street, you will notice how many different building styles from the fifteenth century on can be seen on either side of this single street. In the eighteenth century, coffee houses lined the street. Now its shop fronts with their bay windows retain its character. Half way along at Number 17 is the fifteenth-century **Mulberry Hall** with its overhanging second-story bay windows, which are leaded with diamond-shaped panes.

In a few yards you will come to the sign of **Ye Olde Starre Inn,** one of the few inn-signs in England built across the street. Turn left down an alley to visit this colorful pub. On returning to Stonegate, you may wish to finish this interesting walk through old York by browsing about the many delightful shops on either side of this fascinating street and then to top it off, stroll a few yards beyond the end of Stonegate for a final look at the Minster, to which you will always return while visiting York.

NORWICH

Norwich has an unusual appeal and possesses one of the truly glorious cathedrals in England. It is off the usual tourist route—in East Anglia northeast of London—and consequently relatively unknown to American visitors. In addition to its magnificent cathedral—which alone justifies your visit—Norwich's medieval streets and byways will fascinate you. In the old corner of the city, you will find twisting lanes leading to tiny courtyards and picturesque houses. As you wander about the city, you will encounter Georgian mansions, medieval churches, ancient byways, and attractive Tudor buildings.

Norwich is an important manufacturing center and the commercial capital of the fertile farming country of East Anglia. Founded by the Saxons, Norwich (whose name means "North Town") became famous during the fourteenth to late eighteenth centuries as the principal center of the weaving trade in England. (The name of worsted cloth comes from the nearby village of Worstead in Norfolk.) During the seventeenth and eighteenth centuries Norwich ranked in size next to Bristol and London.

It is easy to reach Norwich. By fast train it is only two hours from London. If you are motoring in eastern England, Norwich is about an hour and a half from Cambridge. The Norfolk Broads are half an hour's drive.

Begin your walking tour of **Norwich** at the **Castle.** Perched on a lofty mound covered with daffodils in springtime, the Castle commands a sweeping view over the city. Here you can get a good idea of old and modern Norwich through which you will wind your way to the superb **cathedral**—a fitting goal to which you can look forward with eager anticipation.

The **Castle Museum** (open weekdays, 10:00–5:00; closing,

151

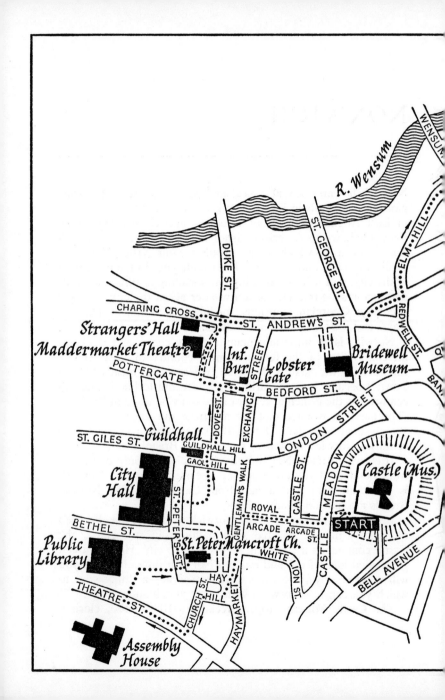

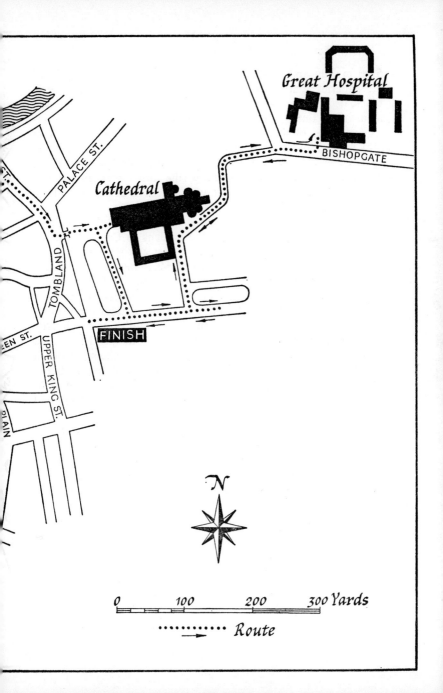

5:30 in July and August, Sundays, 2:30–5:00), a collection of art galleries, natural history, Saxon, Roman, and prehistoric relics, occupies most of the present castle, which had been used as a prison until 1883. The exhibit of **landscape paintings** includes artists of the Norwich school and is worth seeing. You also may enjoy the **Norfolk Room,** showing in dioramas the county's wild birds and animals in their natural surroundings. The twelfth-century **Norman keep** (the fifth largest in Britain) is part of the museum and contains collections of pottery, silver, glass, and armor.

After visiting the Museum and strolling around the Castle to view the city, go down through the gardens to **Castle Meadow,** a wide street lined with shops. Cross over and go left for a few yards, then walk through the **Royal Shopping Arcade** to the large **Market Place.** Here the open stalls displaying farm produce and flowers may remind you of outdoor markets in Holland. You will return later to the far side of the market for a more leisurely look, so turn left on the Walk until you reach **Hay Hill,** an open square on your right. Sir Thomas Browne, a prominent Norwich physician and doctor during the seventeenth century, whose statue is in the Haymarket, is often remembered for his quotation: "Charity begins at home." Next, turn right at the far side of the square, then left on Church Street, and right on Theatre Street.

On your left you are approaching the **Norwich Assembly House** (open 11:00–8:00 except Sunday), the finest example of Georgian architecture in the city. Set back from the street, the brick building is used for city functions as well as by artistic and cultural groups. You will be impressed by the dignity and grace of its entrance and banqueting halls. Note the lovely glass chandelier and the spacious foyer and the artistic paneling and decorative plaster work.

Opposite the Assembly House you will see on your left the modern **public library** of Norwich. After passing it, turn right on **Bethel Street** to the **Church of St. Peter Mancroft.** This fifteenth-century Perpendicular-style parish church is one of the most splendid and largest in all of England. Immediately, you have a strong impression of brightness because of the simple architectural design and the huge windows that flood the church with light. Even the beautiful wooden roof is illuminated by the clerestory windows. Don't miss the lovely medieval glass in the **east window,** created by East Anglian glass painters. Ask to see the collection of **church plate,** one of the finest in the country. While you are here, you may be fortunate enough to hear the bells peal in the massive tower.

The name Mancroft comes from the Latin *Magna Crofta* or Great Meadow.

Turn right from the church and stroll through the fascinating market place. After browsing about the open stalls stroll past Norwich's huge modern **city hall** to the ancient **Guildhall** standing in the middle of a main street (open weekdays, 2:00–4:30). The quaint flintstone building was used as a prison during the fifteenth century. Its **council chamber** is most attractive with its carved oak ceiling and linenfold paneling. One exhibit is the sword which the Spanish Admiral surrendered to Admiral Lord Nelson after the Battle of Cape St. Vincent in 1797. Nelson's portrait, hanging on the wall, is the last one painted before his death at Trafalgar.

Just beyond the Guildhall, go down narrow **Dove Street,** then turn right at the next corner and in a few yards you will reach on your left the office of the Norwich Publicity Association (open 10:00–4:30; Saturdays, 12:30) where helpful information that will add to the enjoyment of your visit is freely available.

Retrace your steps along Pottergate to **St. John Maddermarket Church.** Just beyond it turn sharply to the right down a lane and in a few yards on your left you will see the **Maddermarket Theatre.** In this reproduction of an Elizabethan theatre, the Norwich Players, one of the most famous amateur repertory companies in England, produces one play a month. Its programs encompass Tennessee Williams as well as Shakespeare.

A few steps beyond the theatre you will pass old pastel-colored cottages, with second stories overhanging a tiny square. This is one of the most charming corners of Norwich. Turn left on **Charing Cross** and in a moment on your left you will come to **Strangers' Hall** (open weekdays, 10:00–5:00). In this exceptionally intriguing house, now a museum, you can see rooms illustrating five hundred years of English domestic life from the early fourteenth century undercroft to the Victorian dining and sitting rooms. This is the most interesting house open to tourists in Norwich. The building itself was a medieval merchant's town mansion and possibly called Strangers' Hall after Protestant refugees from the Netherlands at the time of Elizabeth I. Inside you will be intrigued by the rooms furnished in the different periods. The fifteenth-century **banqueting hall,** with its high ceiling, fine room, linenfold paneled screen and old furniture, is exceptionally distinguished. Both the oak paneled room on the ground floor and the delightful Georgian dining room overlooking the walled garden are most attractive and interesting. Be sure to see the cellars with an exhibit of **inn signs** and the **coach house** with the Lord Mayor's coach still in use on important civic occasions. Also step into the **garden,** which is charming.

On leaving Strangers' Hall, turn right along Charing Cross and continue on **St. Andrew Street** as far as the **Church of St. Andrew. Bridewell Alley** turns off at right angles from the street and runs beside the church for a few yards to the **Bridewell Museum** on your left (open weekdays, 10:00–5:00). Pause for a moment in the little courtyard planted with flowers in front of the entrance. In this house, which dates from about 1360, there is a **museum of local industries**—old agricultural implements, examples of Norfolk rush weaving, exhibits of thatched roof construction, the loom on which Queen Victoria's household linen was woven, etc.

Return to St. Andrew Street, then turn right past the church and across the square to **St. Andrew's Hall.** In the fifteenth century this was the nave of the Dominican friars' church and then became a civic hall about two hundred years go. The hall and its cloisters are fine examples of Perpendicular architecture. **Blackfriars' Hall** (adjacent) was a church used by refugee Fleming Protestants in the Elizabethan period.

Opposite St. Andrew's Hall you will see a white stucco house at the junction of two streets. This is **Garsett House,** often called Armada House because some of its beams are reputed to have come from ships of the Spanish Armada. Note its carved wooden corner posts. If you are curious about ancient Norwich, step inside to the offices of the **Norwich Archeological Society.**

Keeping Garsett House on your right, walk just a few yards on **Princes Street** to **St. Peter Hungate Church** on your left at the corner of **Elm Hill** (open weekdays, 10:00–5:00). It is now a museum of religious art. Beneath the church's fine hammer-beam roof you will find an intensely interesting collection. In addition to many beautifully illustrated fourteenth- and fifteenth-century **manuscripts,** the rarest treasure is one section of the John Wyclif's Bible (the other part is in the British Museum). The fifteenth-century **brasses** are fascinating. One macabre exhibit is an oak coffin containing the bones of a person interred during the fourteenth century.

Now stroll down **Elm Hill**—Norwich's unique cobbled street lined with quaint pastel-colored houses restored as they were in Elizabethan days and now occupied by antique shops, booksellers, and art galleries. Deservedly famous, Elm Hill is a perfect delight. Almost every few feet you will stop to admire this medieval house or that little court as you follow the narrow street that curves like an S. There is more atmosphere of medieval Norwich in Elm Hill than anywhere else except the cathedral.

A few yards along Elm Hill past St. Peter Hungate will bring you to the tiny central square shaded by a huge elm tree. Just at the corner on your right is the **Briton's Arms,** a fifteenth-century, timbered building with a thatched roof. At the time of Edward III it was known as "le Godes House" and was inhabited by women who had taken religious vows. Now this charming house, painted in Suffolk pink (a characteristic color in East Anglia that varies from salmon to russet), is a coffee shop where you can enjoy an excellent snack lunch in charming intimate surroundings. If you cannot be here at lunch time, stop in for a morning coffee or afternoon tea.

Many of the houses along Elm Hill belonged to wealthy medieval merchants who often had their workshops in the rear. Opposite the Briton Arms is the **Elm Hill Craft Shop,** a fascinating house with an overhanging second story. As you stroll on the old cobbles along the street, each view of these quaint houses will seem more artistic than the next. The **Stamp Corner** on the square is painted pea green and **Number 20** on the left a robin's egg blue. When Elm Hill was restored, the selection of colors for the houses was decided by city officials. To study the houses in detail, buy the **Guide to Elm Hill.**

On the left the house at Numbers 22 to 26, now the **Strangers' Club,** has a most attractive Tudor timbered front with patterned brickwork and many leaded windows on the second story overlooking the street. If you can get inside, you will see upstairs a superb sixteenth-century room with the most magnificent ceiling in the city. On the opposite side turn into **Norris Court** at Numbers 37–39 to see the charming **rose garden** with lavender border behind the old buildings. Just on your right as you come out of the court is **Numbers 41 and 43,** a distinguished half-timbered house with dormer window that belonged to the Pettus family prominent in Norwich during the Elizabethan period.

Crossing the street again, look at **Number 32,** an attractive pale pink house, now the studio of a portrait photographer, E. Johnson Taylor. Since few of the Elm Hill houses are available to the visitor, you should step inside this one and ask to see that part of the building that was a monastery during the fourteenth century. Upstairs is a long gallery used by weavers during the fifteenth century. Note its old timbers and leaded windows. The church on the corner, **St. Simon and St. Jude,** is fourteenth- or fifteenth-century Perpendicular style.

You will now come into **Wensum Street.** Just across the street slightly to your right is the **Maid's Head Hotel,** an ancient hostelry and tavern since the days of Edward III. Just past the hotel you will be in a tree-shaded square called **Tombland**—a market place, not a graveyard. Its name comes from the Saxon "Toom," meaning open land. Have a look in **Tombland Alley** just by the picturesque seventeenth-century **Samson and Hercules House** on your right.

You have now reached the culmination of your walking tour of Norwich, the magnificent **cathedral** (open 8:00–6:00; from June to September until 7:00 or 8:00). From Tombland turn into its main entrance opposite the Samson and Hercules House —the elaborate, stone **Erpingham Gate,** built by the commander of the English archers at the Battle of Agincourt. As you go through the gate, the towering cathedral spire looms directly ahead. Inside the close you see on your left the old **Grammar School,** which was attended by the noted Elizabethan lawyer Sir Edward Coke and later by Admiral Lord Nelson whose statue stands by the green.

Norwich Cathedral was founded in 1096 by Bishop Herbert de Losinga and is one of the finest examples of Norman work in the country. When you enter, you will be greatly impressed by the splendid proportions of the exceptionally long **nave** and the exquisite beauty of the **triple arcade** of white stone. Light usually floods the cathedral through the windows of the **clerestory.** Look up at the superb **vaulting** of the stone roof. Step into the choir to see the lovely fifteenth-century **choir stalls** and amusing carving on the **misericord seats.** Behind the altar stands the **Bishop's Throne,** older than the cathedral, made of stone and the only one of its kind north of the Alps. Now go into the delightful **cloisters** which are the largest and perhaps the most beautiful left in England.

After sauntering about these quiet cloisters, leave the cathedral through the **south transept,** then turn left for a few yards. The lawn at the rear of the cathedral is called **Life's Green.** Here you will find the stone marking the grave of **Edith Cavell** who was shot during the First World War for helping British prisoners escape. Now look up at the cathedral's great **flying buttresses.**

As you follow the lane at the rear of the cathedral, past the attractive little houses of the close, turn back now and again for views of the tapering spire. At the end of the lane go through the gate to **Bishopsgate** and in a few yards turn left into the grounds of the thirteenth-century **Great Hospital,** one of England's oldest and most beautiful homes for the aged. At the right side of the driveway (where you get another fine view of the spire), pass beneath a brick arch to the charming fifteenth-century **cloister.** Wander about the hospital and then retrace your steps back to the cathedral. After passing the cloister on your right, you will reach **the close** with its stately early Georgian red brick houses. Turn right and in a few moments you will come to the **Upper Close,** an oblong green tastefully planted with birch and cherry trees. Saunter about this tranquil corner of the cathedral grounds. Just before you go through the **Ethelbert Gate** to return to Tombland and the busy city, stop for a moment to admire on your left the lovely Queen Anne houses facing **Almary Green,** a delightful scene on which to end this walking tour of Norwich.

CAMBRIDGE I

Compared to Oxford, **Cambridge** is much the same and yet so different. The center of a rich agricultural area, the city of Cambridge contrasts with Oxford, the city of the Morris automobile works.

Oxford colleges take pride in their quads; Cambridge colleges glory in their **Backs,** those superb gardens and lawns that join one another along the banks of the Cam. Stone is the characteristic of the Oxford quad; brick the hallmark of Cambridge. To have visited Oxford does not mean that Cambridge will be merely a repetition, for in many ways Cambridge is the more beautiful. Rather, one will whet your appetite for the other.

Begin your walk through Cambridge at the largest college of all, **Trinity.** Pause for a few minutes on **Trinity Street** before the tremendous Tudor gate which will prepare you for the vast splendor of Trinity—its front court, chapel, hall, and library. Thomas Nevile, Master of Trinity (1593–1615), who largely built the college as it stands today, conceived his plans on a grand scale. The early fifteenth-century gate is older than the college Henry VIII founded. It formerly marked the entrance to King's Hall, one of the three foundations that preceded Trinity. (All the colleges are open all day unless otherwise noted.)

Inside you face the huge early seventeenth-century **quad**— its sheer size as well as beauty is somewhat staggering. Bigger than any other quad in either Cambridge or Oxford, Trinity will impress you by the beauty of its Tudor-Gothic style. Directly ahead, Nevile's exquisite stone **fountain** plays in the center of the great lawn. To the right of the Gate the **staircase** marked "E" is where Sir Isaac Newton occupied rooms on the first floor

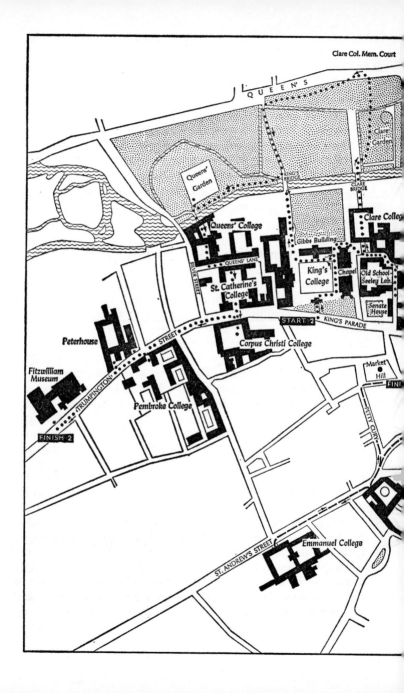

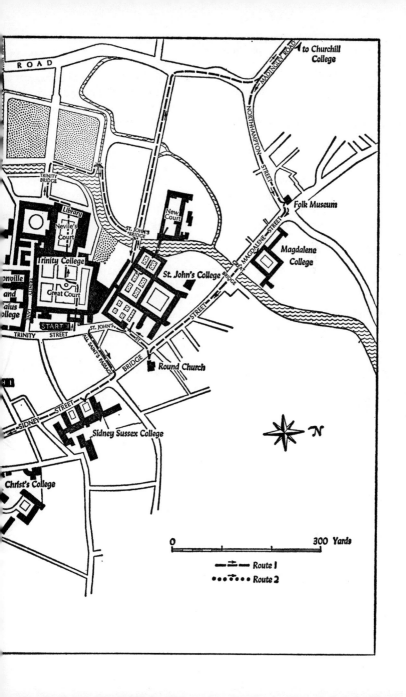

when he formulated the proofs of his great scientific discoveries.

Trinity's dignified **chapel** is also on your right and adjoins the clock tower. Roubiliac's superb **statue of Newton** dominates the antechapel. It is considered possibly the finest work of art in Cambridge.

The medieval **clock tower** was built at the time of the battle of Agincourt. The clock itself strikes the hour twice. At noon this lasts forty-three seconds. Undergraduates often test their speed by attempting to circle the 383 yards around the court before the clock stops striking. You will see an Elizabethan tower in **Merton Corner**—to your left as you face the court from the gate. Here Byron, while a student at Trinity, kept a tame bear.

The flight of steps at the far side of the Great Court from the gate leads to the entrance to **the Hall.** A magnificent Elizabethan hall, it is one of the finest in England. You will admire its hammerbeam oak roof and fine decorative paneling above the High Table from which hangs a splendid copy of Holbein's portrait of Henry VIII. Don't miss Reynolds' charming painting of the Duke of Gloucester at the end of the dais. Another interesting portrait is that of Francis Bacon painted on wood. Look back towards the elaborate woodwork of the **Minstrels Gallery.**

Turn right along the **"Screens" passage,** lined with lovely linenfold paneling, to **Nevile's Court.** Cloisters enclose three sides of the classical court with its strong Italian influence. Wren created one of his masterpieces in his design of the **library** whose noble facade of slightly pinkish stone rises above the loggia.

At the far right-hand corner you go up a flight of steps to the library (open weekdays, 2:30–3:30). Its interior, beautifully proportioned, "touches the very soul of anyone who first sees it" Roger North wrote in 1695 after its completion. Wren even designed the tall bookcases as well as tables and chairs in the alcoves. Grinling Gibbons' carvings of the shelves and walls are superb examples of his best work. At the far end of the library you can see part of Newton's private book collection and diaries. The library's treasures include John Milton's hand-written manuscripts of his shorter poems, and many rare illuminated manuscripts.

From the library stroll to the Backs and cross **Trinity Bridge** to **the Avenue**—one of the best known walks in Cambridge. From the bridge you have a memorable vista in either direction—St. John's on your right and the Backs of other colleges on your left. Pause for a moment on the other side of the bridge and look back at the stately library with the river and green lawn in the foreground.

Turn right on the footpath beside the willows that shade the punt-filled river. In a moment you will have a grand view of the tower of **St. John's Chapel.** Shortly you cross an iron bridge into **St. John's garden.** Go left and then cross another iron bridge. The stone building to your right beyond the lawn—as smooth as a putting green—is **St. John's New Court.** Continue along a line of lime trees and just over another bridge turn right past St. John's garden.

In a moment you can be on **Queen's Road.** Turn right for about a hundred yards and then go left on **Madingley Road** on your way to visit Cambridge's newest college, Churchill, about a ten-minute walk on your right.

Churchill College, officially opened in June 1964 as a national memorial to Sir Winston Churchill, plans to train some 500 students particularly (about 70 percent) in science and technology. One-third of the junior members are advanced students and of this number half come from overseas.

The college buildings are modern in design, built of Stamford-stone brick, grayish brown in color. Churchill's concrete and brick construction contrasts with the customary stone and brick in most Cambridge colleges. You will be interested to look about the series of residential courts connected by covered walks, which make a continuous **internal cloister.** The distinguished roof of the large **dining hall** consists of three reinforced concrete barrel vaults. As you go up the stairway to see the impressive interior of the hall, you will pass a striking bust of Churchill by Oscar Nemon. The **combination and lounge rooms** are attractively but simply decorated. The **library** has been named after Ernest Bevin.

Return along Madingley Road, then bear left on **Northampton Street.** On the corner of **Castle Street** is the **Cambridge Folk Museum** (open Tuesday–Saturday, 11:00–1:00; 2:30–4:30; Sunday, 2:30–4:30). It consists of exhibits depicting the trades, occupations, and domestic crafts illustrating the life and work of Cambridge people from medieval times. There are also several children's rooms and exhibits of rural life.

Turn right into **Magdalene Street** (pronounced Maudlin). In a few yards on your left you pass a row of old houses with projecting stories, bay windows, and russet-tiled steep hipped roofs. On entering **Magdalene College** through the late sixteenth-century gateway you will be in the first court. The old red brickwork has recently been cleaned and the crests have been repainted, giving the buildings a fresh appearance. There is a charming, intimate feeling about this court, part of which on your right was once a fifteenth-century Benedictine abbey. Continue to the second court to visit the famous **Pepys Library** (open 11:30–12:30; 2:30–3:30 in term). It is above the arcade of the lovely English Renaissance building. Pepys' fascinating books are kept in the original oak shelves he had made for them. His collection also includes the manuscript volumes of his diary. Stroll around the charming **garden** to the left of the Pepys building. Its informality and beautiful flowers, especially its exquisite roses, make it one of the most delightful in Cambridge.

Returning to Magdalene Street, you turn left to cross the **Great Bridge** over **the Cam,** the shallowest point where the river could be forded. This is the place from which Cambridge gets its name—the bridge over the Cam.

A bit further on your left and you will come to the **Round Church,** landscaped by a little rose garden. The oldest of only four round churches in England, it dates from the crusaders (1130) and was planned after the Church of the Holy Sepulchre in Jerusalem.

Cross **Bridge Street** and on your right you will face the second most imposing **gate tower** in Cambridge, **St. John's.** The massive dark red brick and stone tower is emblazoned with the brilliantly painted and gilded Tudor rose, and the shield of the founder, Lady Margaret Beaufort, mother of Henry VII. Inquire at the porter's lodge on the right of the gatehouse for permission to see the magnificent **Combination Room.** This **Long Gallery,** now nearly one hundred feet long, has oak paneled walls on which hang exquisite silver sconces dating from 1800. The lovely plaster late eighteenth-century ceiling and Chippendale furniture complete the decoration of probably the most beautiful room of any Oxford or Cambridge college. On your way to the Combination Room you pass through the **college hall.** Its highly decorated hammerbeam roof, **minstrel's gallery,** and fifteenth-century linenfold paneling are among its fine features.

The recent cleaning of St. John's second court adds to the beauty of the fine Elizabethan brickwork. During the renovation the **Tudor Tower** at the far side of the court was largely rebuilt with the original bricks. Proceed through the third court to the **Bridge of Sighs** (somewhat similar to the one in Venice) and to the **New Buildings.** The college **library** with many interesting manuscripts is in the third court and has an **oriel window** overlooking the river. On your way back to the main gate there is a fine vista through the archways of the three courts.

Opposite St. John's gate go down a narrow passageway next to a tiny churchyard and turn left in **All Saint's Passage.** The area on the left was Cambridge's ancient Jewry. On reaching **Sidney Street** cross over and shortly you will come to **Sidney Sussex College.** Stop in for a few minutes to see the pastel painting of Oliver Cromwell, an old member. This portrait is the famous one showing the wart on his face. His skull is buried near the entrance to the chapel.

Continue along busy Sidney Street, usually crowded with shoppers, for a few hundred yards to **Christ's College** on your left. Before you enter, look at the early **Tudor gateway.** It is similar in elaborate decoration to St. John's, with the same Beaufort "Yales," for both were founded by Lady Margaret Beaufort. **John Milton,** the college's most distinguished old

member, occupied rooms on the first floor of the first staircase
—immediately to your left in the front court. **Darwin's** room
was to the right of the gatehouse. Stroll into the garden to see
the **mulberry tree** Milton is supposed to have planted. This
garden, one of Cambridge's loveliest, is particularly outstanding for the variety of its trees and shrubs as well as for its
herbaceous borders.

Stroll along **St. Andrew's Street** a block further to **Emmanuel
College.** John Harvard, the founder of Harvard University, lived
in the old court. His former room is now occupied by a different visiting student from Harvard every year. Across the front
court stands Wren's classical **chapel** behind the loggia. Its quiet
dignity and simplicity is typical of Wren's work. In the chapel
entrance there is a brass plaque commemorating "John Harvard,
A.M. a member of Emmanuel College who emigrated to Massa-
chusetts Bay and there dying in 1638 bequeathed to a college
newly established by the general court his library and one half
his estate wherefore his name is borne by Harvard college that
eldest of the seminaries which advance learning and perpetuate
it to prosperity throughout America." A full-length portrait of
John Harvard appears in a nearby stained-glass window. Wander
behind the southern loggia to the **garden** where you will find a
large pond.

Return along St. Andrew's Street to **Petty Cury**, a narrow
street that bears to the left just after you pass Christ's College.
A minute or two along Petty Cury will lead you to **Market Hill,**
a shopping center since the Middle Ages. Here on market days
vendors display flowers, fruits, vegetables, and miscellaneous
articles on open stalls. This is a good place to end your first
walk through the ancient colleges and beautiful gardens of Cambridge—only a few yards from King's Parade.

CAMBRIDGE II

Start this walk through the enchanting courts and scenic Backs of the colleges at **King's Parade** opposite **King's College.** Stroll in front of the college until you reach a point where you can look across the street at the great Gothic stone screen with its heavily pinnacled gatehouse and see soaring above it the towering glory of **King's College Chapel.**

Before entering the chapel, walk to the left around the **Great Court** with its central fountains surmounted by a statue of Henry VI, the college's founder. Near the gate you may be amused by this little notice on the lawn: "Please do not walk on the grass unless accompanied by a senior member of the college." Continue past Gibbs' fine eighteenth-century **Fellows building** and the wonderful lawn on the far side that slopes down to the river. In a few moments you will reach **King's Bridge** over the Cam. To your right along the stream are the lovely seventeenth-century stone arches and balustrade of **Clare Bridge,** undoubtedly one of the most graceful ever designed. In the distance luxurious trees with a richness only possible in the English climate spread their boughs over the languid Cam. Just across the bridge you have a superb view of King's Chapel looming through the trees above the broad expanse of lawn. Here is a place to sense the contemplative atmosphere and calm, unhurried air that so characterizes the Backs and gives Cambridge its unique quality.

Wander back over the bridge to the Great Court and approach the chapel, often called the noblest Gothic monument and finest example of Perpendicular style in England (open weekdays, 10:00–6:00; Sundays, 10:00–5:00). Commenced by Henry VI in 1446, the chapel was completed in 1515.

After stepping inside the south door you will at once feel humbled by the magnificently proportioned interior. As you glance down the great nave, the beauty of the lofty lacelike **fan vaulting** in stone is extraordinary. The great **rood screen,** considered one of the finest pieces of woodwork in northern Europe, is surmounted by the organ with its four graceful angels. Inquire when the next service will be held and return, if possible, to hear the world-renowned **King's College Choir** in this incomparable setting.

The huge **windows** are the largest and most complete series of ancient windows in the world. You should obtain the booklet that describes them in detail. Made between 1515 and 1531 by both Flemings in England and Englishmen, they represent the best example of Flemish Renaissance **glass painting.** To appreciate their beautiful detail, you should study one or two single figures.

You will want to wander about the various **chantry chapels** and also examine the excellent woodwork of the **choir stalls** and the painting by Rubens of the Adoration of the Magi before you have a last look at this inspiring chapel.

From the west door, stroll to the right around the end of the chapel and after leaving the grounds of King's continue along the street for about fifty yards. The **Old Schools,** former lecture rooms, are on your right. Opposite **Trinity Hall** turn right into **Senate House passage** for a closer view of Gibbs' eighteenth-century classic building. If you are lucky, the **Senate House** on your right will be open. This is the building where the chief university functions, including the meetings of the governing council, are held. The plaster ceiling in English rococo style is one of this handsome building's fine features. From the little square in front of the Senate House you have another exciting view of the front of King's and its interesting gargoyles.

On returning to the Senate House passage, you are facing the Renaissance **Gate of Honor** of **Gonville and Caius** (pronounced "Keys") **College.** Blue and gold sundials decorate the cupola. Go through this gate into the simple court with a charming clock tower on the far side. On the right is the **Gate of**

Virtue which, according to the plan of the college's benefactor, Dr. Caius, the student traversed after entering the **Gate of Humility** on Trinity Street and before leaving the Gate of Honor to get his degree in the Senate House.

Return along Senate House passage to **Trinity Lane.** If you happen to be here in the morning during term, ask to see the beautiful **library.** Turn along Trinity Lane towards King's and in a few yards enter **Clare College** through the fine iron gates. Stroll through the college courts on your way to Clare Bridge. Just before you reach the river you will pass lovely gardens on either side of the path. Pause for a few moments on **Clare Bridge,** the oldest in Cambridge (1640), with its row of stone balls, for another glance up and down the Cam. This is one of the most idyllic scenes in Cambridge—the punts and boats gliding along the still waters of the Cam under the luxuriant trees, the close-cropped grass banks bordering the narrow stream, and the superb gardens. Just to your right on the far side of the bridge through handsome eighteenth-century iron grill gates resplendent with Clare's crest is probably the most beautiful **garden** of all.

A few yards along the path will bring you to its entrance down a few stone steps (open 2:00–5:00 except Saturday and Sunday). To stroll through this exquisitely laid-out and maintained garden is one of the most delightful experiences in all of Cambridge. Wander down to the river for a view of Clare Bridge. Circular flower beds, shrubs, and trees are so carefully landscaped that the combination of colors and arrangement of groupings is quite marvelous. Then stroll along the deep herbaceous border, so artistic in gold and blue. This leads to a sunken garden enclosed by a yew hedge—just the spot to sit for a while and revel in this exceptionally lovely garden.

From Clare Garden saunter down the tree-lined walk to **Queen's Road** and cross over for a look at the new **University Library,** the tall tower behind Clare's Memorial Court. Returning to Queen's Road, turn right along a footpath. After passing the gate to King's go left across the Common to **Silver Street.** Just before you reach the Silver Street bridge you enter the grounds of **Queens' College** on your left. Here is a delightful little walk along the banks of the Cam for a couple of hundred yards and at the end a picturesque view of the river, the graceful arches of King's and Clare bridges, and even a corner of King's Chapel.

On your way back the **Queens' garden** and charming timber and stucco Tudor building of the **President's Lodge** face you on the other side of the Cam. Cross the popularly-named "**Mathematical Bridge**" (alleged to be so-called because of the careful calculation of strains in its construction) to **Queens' Cloister Court.** The combination of the mellow deep red brick medieval building with its arched windows above the cloister, the fine oriel windows and facade of the half-timbered President's Lodging and the high brick wall of the Hall, make this court a perfect gem. Pause for a few minutes in these glorious surroundings to admire the way the superb maroon color of the brick and the sixteenth-century black and white of the President's Lodging seem to blend, though so different. Cloister Court has an intimate, restful charm that is quite unique in Cambridge.

A passageway will lead you to the other side of the President's Lodgings and the new **Erasmus building** in honor of the college's most distinguished old member. This modern building is ingeniously designed. By supporting the building on brick arches and stone pillars and eliminating a ground floor, the architect has preserved a relatively uninterrupted view of the gardens, lawns, and the river bank.

Return to Cloister Court and go into **Queens' Hall,** highly colorful with its medieval decoration and sixteenth-century ceiling. On your way through the first court, dating from 1451, note the elaborate **sundial** below the clock high up under the cupola. Here again you will be impressed by the beauty of the brickwork. Leave Queens' through the original wooden doors of the turreted fifteenth-century gateway.

Cross **Queens' Lane** and stroll through the court of **St. Catharine's College** to **Trumpington Street** and **Corpus Christi College** on the opposite side. The **Old Court,** to your left as you enter the college, is one of the treasures in Cambridge. Completed in 1377, the Old Court is the earliest example of a complete medieval quadrangle still standing. You will be fascinated by its ancient doorways and medieval windows. Also have a look at the spacious **hall** but especially the **library** (open in term, 2:00–4:30) for its great collection of early printing and priceless manuscripts. The porter at the lodge will direct you to the room **Christopher Marlowe** occupied.

Turn left from Corpus' gate along Trumpington Street and in a couple of minutes you will reach **Pembroke College.** Stop in to see **Wren's chapel,** one of his earliest works. Its simplicity, excellent proportions and large windows give it a dignified air and will remind you of some of Wren's churches in the City of London.

A bit further along Trumpington Street on the opposite side is the **Church of St. Mary the Less,** which dates from 1350. Americans will be greatly interested in a memorial tablet to the left of the entrance commemorating Rev. Godfrey Washington, a former minister of the church and a relative of George Washington. The family coat of arms above the memorial with its red and silver stripes and three red stars was the origin of the American flag. Don't miss the attractive little cottages along **St. Mary's Lane.**

Peterhouse, founded in 1284 and the oldest college in Cambridge, stands next to St. Mary the Less. Just inside the front court you will see the seventeenth-century **chapel** with a classical loggia on either side—an unusual architectural design. The **hall** and **buttery** in the old court are substantially as they were in the thirteenth century. Just beyond the Hall you can enter Peterhouse's extensive **gardens.** Wander through the gardens to see the new eight-story modern dormitory building, one of the best in Cambridge and sometimes called Peterhouse's skyscraper.

You should end this tour of Cambridge by visiting the **Fitzwilliam Museum** (open weekdays, 10:00–5:00; picture gallery only, Sunday 2:00–5:00; closes 4:00 September 1–April 30) just a few yards beyond Peterhouse. The spacious and well-lighted Fitzwilliam galleries contain one of the finest collections of art and antiquities outside London. Although the museum's department of Egyptian, Greek, Roman, and medieval art is outstanding, including notable exhibits of coins, pottery, porcelain, and medieval manuscripts, you may be particularly interested in the paintings and prints. The Italian, Dutch, and English schools are well represented and the Fitzwilliam also possesses an unusually interesting selection of French impressionists.

Here, in these artistic surroundings, you can try and decide which colleges you want to revisit on your next trip to Cambridge.